Student Workbook

for

D1560490

Social Work Research Methods
Qualitative and Quantitative Approaches

W. Lawrence Neuman
University of Wisconsin-Whitewater

Larry W. Kreuger
University of Missouri-Columbia

Boston   New York   San Francisco
Mexico City   Montreal   Toronto   London   Madrid   Munich   Paris
Hong Kong   Singapore   Tokyo   Cape Town   Sydney

ISBN   0-205-38685-7

Printed in the United States of America

10 9 8 7 6 5 4 3 2 1   08 07 06 05 04 03 02

TABLE OF CONTENTS

TO THE STUDENT

Each chapter has a list of learning objectives, the list of key terms with definitions for matching, and exercises. The following are suggestions to help you learn the material and study a chapter:

1. First, review the Chapter Outline in the textbook to get a general idea of what the chapter covers.
2. Read through the entire chapter slowly from beginning to end. Read subheadings and take notes on key ideas, terms or principles by restating them in your own words or with your own examples. Also write down questions to bring to your class for discussion.
3. After finishing the chapter, read the list of Key Terms at the end. If there are any that you do not know or about which you are uncertain, go back to find them in the chapter.
4. Read the Review Questions at the end of the chapter and write an answer to each, return to the text if you are uncertain.
5. Get together with another student in the class and discuss the answers to the Review Questions. Do you agree? If not, discuss the differences.
6. Now go to the **Workbook**. First, read the Learning Objectives for the chapter. Can you do each of the things listed? If not, return to the textbook chapter and reread relevant sections.
7. Complete the Matching Key Terms for each chapter. To do this, read each definition and match it to a term without looking at the chapter. Next, go back to the chapter to check your answers.
8. Complete the Exercises assigned by your teacher and any you find of interest.
9. Do the practice quizzes and afterward look up answers in the back of the workbook.
10. If you are serious about social research and find a specific chapter especially interesting read the Recommended Readings section at the end of each chapter and pick one book. See whether your library has a copy of it for you to read.

CHAPTER 1

SCIENCE AND SOCIAL WORK RESEARCH

LEARNING OBJECTIVES

After studying Chapter 1 you will be able to do the following

1. Distinguish between social work research and alternative ways to gain knowledge about the social world, and explain why science is often superior;
2. Understand how the scientific attitude and method apply to the study of the social work settings;
3. Explain what the scientific social work community is, how it operates, and how publications fit into it;
4. Describe major norms of the scientific community and their consequences;
5. Identify and correctly place the steps of social work research in sequence;
6. Understand the meaning of "empirical data;"
7. Distinguish between quantitative and qualitative social work research.

MATCHING DEFINITIONS

1. Ideas or information presented with the jargon and outward appearance of science to win acceptance, but it lacks the systematic rigor of the scientific method.
2. A norm of the scientific community that creating scientific knowledge is a public act, the knowledge belongs to everyone and should be communicated.
2. A norm of the scientific community that irrespective of who conducts research or where it was conducted, it should be judged on its merits alone.
4. Information in the form of words, pictures, sounds, visual images or objects.
5. A set of interconnected ideas that condense, systematize, and organize knowledge about the social world.
6. Events and things that are observable and can be experienced through the human senses (e.g., touch, sight, hearing, smell, taste).
7. A collection of people who share a system of rules and attitudes that sustain the process of producing scientific knowledge.
8. Numerical and non-numerical forms of information and evidence that have been carefully gathered according to rules or established procedures.
9. The tendency to take notice of certain people or events based upon past experience or attitudes.
10. Information in the form of numbers.
11. A norm of the scientific community to be neutral, impartial, receptive, and open-minded to new ideas and not rigidly wedded to a particular point of view.
12. A norm of the scientific community to not accept a new idea or evidence in a carefree, uncritical manner, but to question and subject it to intense scrutiny.
13. A way of thinking about and looking at the world that reflects a commitment to the norms and values of the scientific community.
14. The process of evaluating a social work research report for possible publication in which evaluators do not know the name of the researcher and the researcher does not know who serves as evaluators.
15. The primary form in which new social work research is publicly communicated and made available within the scientific community.

16. The acceptance of broad statements about the situations or events based upon a narrow perspective or very few cases.
17. A tendency to accept information quickly, failing to investigate it to the degree of depth demanded by scientific standards.
18. The process of creating new social work knowledge using the ideas, techniques, and rules of the <u>scientific community</u>.
19. A tendency to allow the positive reputation of people, places or things to "rub off" or color thinking and judgments instead of remaining neutral.

NAME _____ DATE

MATCHING KEY TERMS FOR CHAPTER 1

___	Blind Review	___	Qualitative Data
___	Communalism	___	Quantitative Data
___	Data	___	Scholarly Journal Article
___	Disinterestedness	___	Scientific Attitude
___	Empirical	___	Scientific Community
___	Halo effect	___	Scientific Method
___	Organized Skepticism	___	Selective Observation
___	Overgeneralization	___	Social Theory
___	Premature Closure	___	Universalism
___	Pseudoscience		

Exercise 1.1

Instructions: Telephone or email two university teachers, one in the social work and one in the natural sciences, and arrange meet for 15 minutes. Have an informal conversation with each. Ask how he/she defines "science," how research results get published in his/her field, and ask him/her to describe the review process used for scholarly journal articles (e.g., whether blind review is used). Describe the ideas of universalism and organized skepticism, and ask whether these norms operate in his/her field.

Professor 1:   Department: Date of Degree:

Definition of Science:

How results get published:

Review process for scholarly articles:

Does Universalism Operate?

Does Organized Skepticism Operate?

Professor 2:   Department: Date of Degree:

Definition of Science:

How results get published:

Review process for scholarly articles:

Does Universalism Operate?

Does Organized Skepticism Operate?

EXERCISE 1.2

The Director is considering changing a county welfare office's intake procedures in order to decrease the typical social worker's caseload. She calls in her colleagues to make a decision. The intake worker says, " New intake procedures were tried in a neighboring county, and they didn't work there so they won't work here." The caseworker with the most experience says, "We can't change it because we've had the same procedures for the past 15 years, and they always worked OK before." The Assistant Director says, "My brother is an expert on these matters, and he says it's a good idea." The eligibility officer says, "I've read two articles in <u>Child Welfare</u> on intake procedures, and they prove that the proposed new procedures are always best so we do not need to look any further.."

Which error of non-scientific thinking would be made if the County Director agreed with reasoning of the following? Use the following for your answers: Tradition, Authority, Media Myth, Premature Closure, Selective Observation, Overgeneralization. The reasoning of the Director's colleagues may have more than one error.

Intake Worker?
Explain your answer:

Most experienced Caseworker?
Explain your answer:

Assistant Director?
Explain your answer:

Eligibility Officer?
Explain your answer:

CHAPTER 2

DIMENSIONS OF SOCIAL WORK RESEARCH

LEARNING OBJECTIVES

After studying Chapter 2 you will be able to do the following:
1. Describe the goals of exploratory, descriptive and explanatory research, and recognize study types;
2. Understand basic and applied research and identify at least five areas where they differ;
3. Describe the five types of applied research and explain how each is used;
4. Understand how cross-sectional, time series, panel and case study research differ;
5. Identify a social work research project as being an experiment, a survey, content analysis, existing statistics, field research, or comparative-historical research.

MATCHING DEFINITIONS
1. Social work research in which one studies a few people or cases in great detail over time.
2. A type of qualitative social work research in which a researcher directly observes the people being studied in a natural setting for an extended period. Often by the researcher combines intense observing with participation in their social activities.
3. The idea that chance occurrences or unexpected things can happen that reveal much about the social world.
4. A type of applied social work research in which one tries to determine how well a program or policy is working, or reaching its goals and objectives.
5. Applied social work research in which one collects data to identify problems that require attention and considers the extent and severity of the problems.
6. Longitudinal social work research in which the exact same cases or people are observed at multiple points in time.
7. Social work research like a "snapshot," it looks at a single point in time.
8. A type of evaluation research that occurs after a program or policy being evaluated ends.
9. Social work research which attempts to solve a concrete problem or address a policy question and has a direct, practical application.
10. A technique economists developed in which one assigns events or conditions a monetary value then estimates the positive and negative consequences.
11. Research in which one examines different cultures or periods in time to better understand them.
12. Research to advances basic knowledge on the fundamentals of social relations and develops theoretical explanations.
13. Social work research in which one intervenes or does something to one group of people but not to another, then compares results for the two groups.
14. Research that focuses on why events occur or tries to test and build theory.
15. Quantitative social work research in which one systematically asks many people the same questions, records their answers, then analyzes the answers.
16. Research that always begins in the natural setting, using the human being as the primary data gathering instrument
17. Social work research in which one "paints a picture" with words or numbers, presents a profile, outlines stages, or classifies types.

18. Social work research in which one examines numerical information from government documents or official reports to address new research questions.
19. Social work research on a set of people who share a common experience across time.
20. A type of <u>applied social work research</u> in which the purpose is to facilitate social change or a political-social goal.
21. <u>Applied social work research</u> that documents the consequences for various areas of social life that are likely to result from introducing a major change in a community.
22. Any social work research that takes place over time, in which different people or cases may be looked at in each time point.
23. A type of <u>evaluation research</u> first used by the U.S. Department of Defense, which measures program success based upon its costs and efficiency at reaching preset goals and objectives.
24. Social work <u>evaluation research</u> that occurs throughout the process of program or policy being evaluated.
25. Research into an area that has not been studied and in which a researcher wants to develop initial ideas and a more focused research question.
26. Research that is especially well suited for social work clients who are often marginalized from the mainstream and traditional 'Euro-centered' societies.
27. Research which examines patterns of symbolic meaning within written text, audio, visual or other communication medium.
28. Any research that examines more than one time point.
29. Social work research in which one does not gather data oneself, but re-examines data previously gathered by someone else and asks new questions.
30. Social work research that defines, designs, and implements strategies for effective practice with persons from various cultures and backgrounds

NAME _____ **DATE**

MATCHING KEY TERMS FOR CHAPTER 2

_ Action-Oriented Research
_ Applied Research
_ Basic Research
_ Case-Study Research
_ Cohort Analysis
_ Constructivist Research
_ Content Analysis
_ Cost-Benefit Analysis
_ Cross-Sectional Research
_ Descriptive Research
_ Diversity Research
_ Empowerment Research
_ Evaluation Research
_ Existing Statistics Research
_ Experimental Research
_ Explanatory Research

_ Exploratory Research
_ Field Research
_ Formative Evaluation Research
_ Historical-Comparative Research
_ Longitudinal Research
_ Needs Assessment
_ Panel Study
_ Planning, Programming and Budgeting System
_ Secondary Analysis Research
_ Serendipity
_ Social Impact Assessment
_ Summative Evaluation
_ Survey Research
_ Time Series Research

Exercise 2.1

Instructions: Contact a local agency, public or not-for-profit and interview the president, administrative manager, or executive director. Ask about the types information the agency needs to carry out its programs and activities (e.g., assessment of need in an area, evaluation of how successful a program is). Also ask how often she/he would like the information collected. Next, ask about current applied research that the agency is undertaking to gather the information. Lastly, ask about types of research the organization would like to undertake under ideal conditions, but cannot because of time, money staff shortages or other barriers.

Name of Agency: _____

Name/Title of Person Interviewed:_____

Information Needs:

Current applied research that the agency is undertaking:

Ideally would like to undertake:

Exercise 2.2

The executives of a large state agency were concerned rising health insurance costs and missed work due to health problems among employees who were heavy smokers. The Human Relations Department devised a quit-smoking program and asked Kamisha , one of the social workers, to conduct a study on the agency's 600 employees. In January, she gave a survey questionnaire to each employee that asked about his or her smoking behavior and reactions to a planned program to reduce smoking. In the program all non-smoking employees get a $150 monthly reimbursement check from health insurance savings for a period of three years if they continued to be non-smokers and had no smokers in their household. Each smoking employees was offered one day at full pay to attend a free quit-smoking workshop. They were also eligible for the reimbursement after they went at least six weeks without smoking at all. Once she surveyed all employees, she put the program into operation.

In June after the quit-smoking program had been in operation, Kamisha conducted a second survey of all employees who had been working for the agency in January. She asked what they thought about it. As part of the survey, she asked persons who were smokers in January and who had taken advantage of the program whether they still smoked. In November all employees who had participated in the previous two surveys were surveyed for a third time. Kamisha again asked about their reactions to the program and about their smoking behavior. In December, Kamisha used the results from the three surveys to prepare a report for the Human Resources Department on how well the program worked in reducing employee smoking.

1. Is Kamisha's research Exploratory, Descriptive or Explanatory? What about the description of the study tells you this?

2. Is Kamisha's research basic or applied? If applied, what type of applied is it? What in the description of the study tells you this?

3. Is the study cross-sectional, panel, time series or case study? What in the description of the study tells you this?

Exercise 2.3

Go to your college library or on-line sources that have access to the full texts of articles and look up three scholarly journal articles from the list below (all have been mentioned in Chapter 2 of the textbook). Using the categories in Table 2.2, write a short essay explaining the type of research used in each of the articles you selected. Explain what specific features of the article tell you that it is the type you have identified.

Blythe, B. J., Salley , M. P. & Jayaratnea, S. (1994). A review of intensive family preservation services research. *Social Work Research. 18(4), 213-224.*

Dworkin, J. (1988). To certify or not to certify: Clinical social work decisions and involuntary hospitalization. *Social Work in Health Care.13(4), 81-98.*

Healy, T. C. (2000). Community-dwelling cognitively impaired frail elders: An analysis of social workers' decisions concerning support for autonomy. *Social Work in Health Care. 30(2), 27-47.*

Loewenstein, G. (1985). "The new underclass" *Sociological Quarterly, 26,* 35-48.

Marcenko, M. O. & Samost, L. (1999). Living with HIV/AIDS: The voices of HIV-positive mothers. *Social Work. 44(1), 36-45.*

Marvell, T. & Moody, C.(1995).The impact of enhanced prison terms for felonies committed with guns. *Criminology, 33,*247-82.

South, S. & Lloyd K. (1995). Spousal alternative and marital dissolution. *American Sociological Review, 60,* 126-140.

Orbuch, T. & Esyter, S. (1997). Division of labor among black couples and white couples. *Social Forces 76,* 301-332.

Reece, S. & Levin, B. (1968) Psychiatric disturbances in adopted children: A descriptive study. *Social Work. 13(1), 101-111.*

Toseland, R. W, Kabat, D. & Kemp, K. (1983). Evaluation of a smoking-cessation group treatment program. *Social Work Research & Abstracts. 19(1), 12-19.*

Umberson, D. & Chen, M. (1994). Effects of a parent's death on adult children: Relationship salience and reaction to loss. *American Sociological Review, 59,* 152-168.

Wilhelm, B. (1998). Changes in cohabitation across cohorts: The influence of political activism. *Social Forces, 77,* 289-310.

THEORY AND SOCIAL WORK RESEARCH

LEARNING OBJECTIVES

After studying Chapter 3 you will be able to do the following:
1. Define social work theory and describe how concepts are used in theory;
2. Distinguish between scientific and everyday explanations, prediction, and understanding;
3. Understand classifications and causal relationships in social work theory;
4. Describe how social work theory and research complement one another;
5. Understand differences between micro, meso and macro levels of theorizing;
6. Distinguish between inductive and deductive theory building;
7. Know the three conditions for causality and how to read a simple causal diagram;
8. Understand causal, structural and interpretative explanation.

MATCHING DEFINITIONS

1. Complex, multidimensional concepts that have subtypes. They are parts of <u>social work theories</u> between one simple concept and a full theoretical explanation.
2. A set of closely interrelated ideas with common <u>assumptions</u>, belong to a larger <u>social work theory</u>.
3. A <u>social work theory</u> that prefers treatments such as cognitive therapies, desensitization, consistency of rewards, and token economies.
4. A co-occurrence of two events, factors, characteristics or activities, such that when one happens the other likely to occur as well. Many statistics measure this.
5. The idea that a simple is better. Everything else being equal, a <u>social work theory</u> or argument that can explain more with less complexity is best.
6. A language and set of terms used by a group of people with specialized knowledge or expertise to communicate more quickly and effectively with one another. It may be used inappropriately when experts fail to translate their ideas into ordinary terms for non-specialists or when people are trying to give an impression that they are experts.
7. A statement in <u>social work theory</u> about why events occur that is expressed in terms of causes and effects. They correspond to <u>associations</u> in the <u>empirical</u> world.
8. A statement about something that is likely to occur in the future.
9. Theory that suggests that intervention should involve advocacy, helping clients find, recognize and utilize their own power bases, or by participatory and revolutionary consciousness raising and political action.
10. A pure model about an idea, process or event. One develops it to think about it more clearly and systematically. It is used both as a method of <u>qualitative data</u> analysis and in <u>social theory</u> building.
11. A characteristic of concepts about social reality. They range from the concrete and <u>empirical</u> to very abstract ideas.
12. <u>Theories</u> and explanations about more abstract, large-scale and broad-scope aspects of social reality, such as social change in major institutions (e.g., the family, education) in a whole nation across several decades.
13. <u>Theories</u> and explanations about the concrete, small-scale and narrow level of reality, such as

face-to-face interaction in small groups during a one-month period.

14. Theory that suggests that treatment should involve developing connections, contracting, modifying interactions; collaborating and bargaining.

15. A quasi-theoretical statement that summarizes findings or empirical regularities. It uses few if any abstract concepts and only makes a statement about a reoccurring pattern that researchers observe.

16. A basic statement in social work theory that two ideas or variables are related to one another. It can be true or false (e.g., most sex offenders were themselves sexually abused when growing up), conditional (e.g., if a foreign enemy threatens, then the people of a nation will feel much stronger social solidarity), and/or causal (e.g., poverty causes crime).

17. Theory that recommends that interventions be very practical to deal with and resolve disturbances in people's lives.

18. Parts of theories that are not tested, but act as starting points or basic beliefs about the world. They are necessary to make other theoretical statements and to build theory.

19. The idea that some events occur earlier in time than other events, which is used in evaluating a causal explanation.

20 An approach to inquiry or theory beginning with concrete empirical details, then works toward abstract ideas or principles.

21. Race and/or ethnicity, gender, age, physical/mental abilities, sexual orientation, and size are indicative of this concept.

22. Theory rooted in observations of specific, concrete details.

22. A type of classification with two or more concepts in which the intersection of the concepts creates a set of subtypes or lower-level concepts. Often it is the basis of a concept cluster in theory.

24. Theories and explanations about the middle level of social reality between a broad and narrow scope, such as the development and operation of social organizations, communities, or social movements over a five-year period.

25. A type of theory in which the logic of explanation is not a causal explanation with linear relationships. Instead the logic is one of branching out or a set of interlocked linkages around a central core, like a spider web.

26. An approach to inquiry or theory in which one begins with abstract ideas and principles then works toward concrete, empirical details to test the ideas.

27. Theory that suggests that treatment should involve unconditional positive regard, empathy, non-directive assistance in some perspectives, active planning and prospective community development in others.

28. An association between two variables such that as values on one increase, values on the other also increase.

29. An association between two variables such that as values of one increase, values on the other variable fall or decrease.

30. Social work theory based on biological analogies, in which the social world or its parts are seen as systems, with its parts serving the needs of the system.

31. Variables such as political ideology, geography, marital/family status, socioeconomic status, religion, or occupation/skills, experiences and education comprise this concept.

32. Theory would recommend treatment based on conversation between client and therapist, who functions like a reflective or blank screen

MATCHING KEY TERMS FOR CHAPTER 3

_ Association
_ Assumption
_ Behaviorist-Cognitive Theory
_ Causal Explanation
_ Classification
_ Concept Cluster
_ Crisis Intervention Theory
_ Deductive Approach
_ Empirical Generalization
_ Functional Theory
_ Grounded Theory
_ Humanist/Strengths Theory
_ Ideal Type
_ Inductive Approach
_ Jargon
_ Level of Abstraction

_ Macro-Level
_ Meso-Level
_ Micro-Level
_ Negative Relationship
_ Network Theory
_ Parsimony
_ Positive Relationship
_ Prediction
_ Primary Diversity
_ Proposition
_ Psychodynamic/Functional Theory
_ Secondary Diversity
_ Social Justice/Feminist Theory
_ Systems/Ecological Theory
_ Temporal Order
_ Typology

Exercise 3.1

Develop a typology of types of college students. First, determine the purpose of the typology: Is it for a student who is seeking friends; for a professor organizing thinking about the students she/he encounters; for college administrators to plan for the needs of various types of students; for a residence hall director who wants to assign roommates; or for a recruiter looking for students for a job?

PURPOSE:

Next, decide upon one dimension of the typology (e.g., reasons students attend college, grades students get) and label at least three levels or categories of this dimension.

Decide on a second dimension of the typology and determine at least two levels or categories for this dimension.

Construct the typology by looking at the different combinations of students along the two dimensions. Label or give a name to each combination in the typology. You should have at least six types of students.

Exercise 3.2

Identify a concept, a grouping of people, social role, or organization which you are familiar with (e.g., a church, a family, a rock band, a college professor). Create an ideal type by identifying eight characteristics the ideal model would possess.

IDEAL TYPE OF A(N) _____

1.
2.
3.
4.
5.
6.
7.
8.

Now identify and compare your ideal type to five specific cases you know about. Discuss how well each case fits the ideal type (e.g., which of the eight characteristics does it fit poorly with, which one does it fit well with)?

Case 1   How well does it fit?

Case 2   How well does it fit?

Case 3   How well does it fit?

Case 4   How well does it fit?

Case 5   How well does it fit?

PRACTICE QUIZ 1, Chapters 1-3 (7 questions)

1. Miguel and Michele praise a social work study. Before they had read the study, they
   expected it to be excellent because the study's author is a world-famous scholar in social
   work at a prestigious university. They said anyone like the author who has a job at a top
   university must be correct. Miguel and Michele are violating which norm of the
   scientific community?
   - a. Selective observation
   - b. Organized skepticism
   - c. Communalism
   - d. Universalism
   - e. Disinterestedness

2. Which best describes the goal of **exploratory social work research**?
   - a. Advance knowledge about an underlying process or complete a theory.
   - b. Develop better questions and a direction for future research.
   - c. Give a verbal or numerical (e.g. percentages) picture.
   - d. Extend a theory or principle into new areas or issues.
   - e. Provide evidence to support or refute an explanation.

3. What type of social work study examines at a group of people who share a common life
   experience at the same time, then sees how that experience continues to have an impact
   on their behavior or attitudes?
   - a. Cohort analysis
   - b. Action-oriented research
   - c. Cross-sectional research
   - d. PPBS
   - e. Social Impact Assessment

4. Which of the following is TRUE about an **ideology**, but FALSE about **theory**?
   - a. It contains assumptions and concepts.
   - b. It welcomes empirical tests, and both positive and negative evidence equally.
   - c. It seeks consistency and tries to consider all sides.
   - d. It changes based on evidence and is growing or expanding.
   - e. It is fixed, closed and finished because it already has all the answers.

5 Which of the following would be considered **formal theory**?
   - a. Increased size of human services agencies causes increased specialization of tasks, which
     results in greater formal communication between workers.
   - b. Large agencies that have many social workers have more who specialize in a service or
     intervention
   - c. Social workers who work in small towns are less likely to give as many written
     rules or guidelines on how to do their jobs than are social workers who practice in
     large communities.
   - d. Students in small groups with face-to-face interaction individual students tend to
     shift social roles more often and do more different tasks than when they are in
     huge, impersonal groups.
   - e. Large universities have more rules and regulations on proper student conduct than small
     universities.

6. There are two forms of cost-benefit analysis, in **contingency evaluation cost benefit
   analysis**, a researcher
   - a. Adds up the actual cost of medical bills, time loss at work due to illness, and so forth to
     estimate the costs.

   b. Will charge a cost that is contingent on who does the scientific analysis, no matter who benefits from results.

   c. Makes certain that the people who receive the greatest benefit most pay the highest costs.

   c. Asks people what they would endure for a certain amount of money then totals it for all people to estimate the costs.

   e. Makes sure everyone is equal and that costs and benefits are always in balance.

7. All of the following characterized **applied social work research** <u>EXCEPT</u> which one?
   a. Doing research is usually part of a job assignment and sponsors/supervisors who are not professional researchers themselves will judge and use the findings.

   b. Success is based on whether sponsors/supervisors use the results in decision-making.

   c. The central goal is to produce practical payoffs or uses for the results.

   d. Research problems that one can explore are limited by the interests of an employer or sponsor.

   e. The primary concern is with the internal logic and rigor of the research design, so a social work researcher attempts to reach the very highest levels of scientific rigor and quality of scholarship.

THE MEANINGS OF METHODOLOGY

LEARNING OBJECTIVES

After studying Chapter 4 you will be able to do the following:
1. Understand that there are multiple definitions of social science and major implications of such diversity;
2. Give the definition and major features of positivism;
3. Give the definition and major features of an interpretative approach;
4. Give the definition and major features of a critical science approach;
5. Explain the differences between causal laws and meaningful social action;
6. Contrast how the three approaches see common sense and human nature;
7. Discuss how the value free position in positivism differs from relativism of the interpretative approach and activist stance of critical social science;
8. Provide the major characteristics of Feminist and post-modern social research.

MATCHING DEFINITIONS
1. A German word that translates as understanding, specifically it means an empathic understanding of another's worldview.
2. The ideal that science must be totally objective and based on empirical evidence alone. There is no place for a culture's values or a researcher's personal values or beliefs.
3. An idea in critical social science that social theory and everyday practice interact or work together, mutually affecting one another. This interaction can promote social change. An action-oriented approach to social research.
4. A type of critical social science that advocates action-oriented research. It views the social world as a web of social relations based on mutual obligations, and it rejects positivism as having many assumptions that are male-oriented.
5. A view of the world that is "means-ends" oriented. In it the value of an activity, event or object primarily depends on whether a person can use it to accomplish some other purpose or goal; it has little intrinsic value in itself.
6. An approach to social science that focuses on achieving an understanding of how people create and maintain their social worlds.
7. A very radical approach to social research that eliminates the distinction between artistic expression or subjective experience and science. It deconstructs or takes apart surface appearances; rejects logical reasoning, the ideal that a universal truth exists; and denies the idea of progress or a movement toward more knowledge.
7. The idea that different people will agree on what they observe in the empirical world through careful use of their senses (i.e., touch, sight, hearing).
9. An approach based upon laws, or that operates according to a system of laws.
10. An approach that focuses on creating detailed descriptions of specific events in particular time periods and settings. It rarely goes beyond empirical generalizations to abstract social theory or causal laws.
11. An approach to social science that goes beyond surface illusions to reveal underlying structures and conflicts of social relations as a way to empower people to improve the social world.
12. The idea that there is no single correct way to do things or correct values; rather, every value or point of view is valid for those who hold it.

13. An idea from <u>interpretative social science</u> that for an explanation to be true, the people being studied can understand it, and it "makes sense" to them.
14. An approach that was originally used to study a written text both in detail and as a whole to enable people to see the deeper meanings contained within it. The approach was expanded in <u>interpretative social science</u> to be a method for developing a deeper understanding of events in the social world.
15. Actions that people engage in for subjective reasons or to which other people in a social setting attach significance.
16. An approach to social science that combines a <u>deductive approach</u> with precise measurement of <u>quantitative data</u> so researchers can discover and confirm <u>causal laws</u> that will permit <u>predictions</u> about human behavior.
17. An approach that focuses on getting ordinary things accomplished in the "real" social world of common, everyday affairs.
18. A general organizing framework for <u>social theory</u> and <u>empirical</u> research. It includes basic <u>assumptions</u>, major questions to be answered, models of good research practice and theory, and methods for finding the answers to questions.
19. A form of change emphasized by <u>critical social science.</u> Over time, the organization of a society, social institutions, or relationships contain internal contradictions and deep-seated tensions. The contradictions trigger the destruction of one form of society, institution or relation and transform it into a new, qualitatively distinct form or stage.
20. A view of people embraced by some <u>positivists</u> in which researchers can develop <u>social theories</u> and explanations that are based careful observations of people's external behaviors and their responses to outside forces alone, i.e., without any reference to a mind or consciousness.
21. An <u>assumption</u> that individuals have great freedom to decide and act, and are little affected by external pressures or forces.
22. Basic rules outlined in <u>social theory</u> that identify <u>associations</u> in <u>empirical</u> social reality. They are used by the <u>positivist</u> approach to talk about how events in the social world operate, i.e., in terms of regular, systematic cause-effect relations.
23. An <u>assumption</u> that individuals have little freedom to decide and act, and are controlled by external social pressure or forces.

NAME _____   DATE

MATCHING KEY TERMS FOR CHAPTER 4

____	Causal Laws	____	Nomothetic
____	Critical Social Science	____	Paradigm
____	Determinism	____	Positivist social science
____	Dialectic	____	Post-modern Research
____	Feminist Research	____	Postulate of Adequacy
____	Hermeneutics	____	Practical Orientation
____	Idiographic	____	Praxis
____	Instrumental Orientation	____	Relativism
____	Interpretative Social Science	____	Value Free Science
____	Intersubjectivity	____	*Verstehen*
____	Meaningful Social Action	____	Volunteerism
____	Mechanical Model of Man		

Exercise 4.1

Look at the six common features of the three approaches to the social sciences (Box 4.3) in the textbook, and return to the discussion of the scientific community and its norms in Chapter 1. Which items come from the norms or operation of the scientific community?

Exercise 4.2 (for entire class)

<u>Before class</u>: The instructor writes a scrambled list of the 24 statements from Table 4.1 of the textbook with slight wording changes. Each entry gets a letter in scrambled order. The class into 3-4 person groups which get a list and a copy of the table below.

<u>In class</u>: With books closed, each group tries to place identify which statement corresponds to a space in the table. After all groups have filled the table and written the letter of the entry in the table, a representative from each group copies the information from their table onto a similar blank table written on the black board for the class to see.

	Positivist	Interpretative	Critical
Purpose of Research is . . .			
Social Reality is . . .			
Human Nature is . . .			
Common sense is . . .			
Theory looks like . . .			
Good Explanation is . . .			
Good Evidence is . . .			
The role of Values is . . .			

CHAPTER 5

THE ETHICS AND POLITICS OF SOCIAL WORK RESEARCH

LEARNING OBJECTIVES

After studying Chapter 5 you will be able to do the following,
1. Understand the historical development of ethics in social work research and its origins in specific events;
2. Discuss dilemmas or issues involved in the treatment of human subjects;
3. Understand the pressures on social work researchers who conduct sponsored research and debate ways to respond to such pressures;
4. Explain the role of an IRB, informed consent requirements, and reasons for the requirements;
5. Discuss how political pressures can affect the type of social work research that is conducted;
6. Describe the role of The NASW Code of Ethics and describe the types of items found therein;
7. Discuss studies in the literature that involve significant discussion over the ethics involved;
8. Describe the concept of academic freedom and its importance;
9. Discuss issues in the dissemination of research findings;
10. Distinguish between meanings of value neutrality and objectivity.

MATCHING DEFINITIONS
1. A name for the study by the U.S. Public Health Service that highlighted a failure to protect subjects from physical harm and a failure to obtain <u>informed consent</u>. In the study researchers withheld medical treatment for syphilis for many years from poor black males who were <u>subjects</u> so they could study the disease.
2. A statement, usually written, in which people in a study learn aspects about the project and formally agree to participate.
3. A guarantee that researchers and/or teachers are free to examine all topics and discuss all ideas without any restrictions, threats or interference from people or authorities outside the community of teachers, scholars and scientists.
4. A type of unethical behavior in which a researcher fakes or creates false data, or falsely reports on the research procedure.
5. A type of <u>applied research</u> that is sponsored, i.e., paid for by a government agency, foundation, company, etc. The researcher agrees to conduct a study on the sponsor's research question and finish the study by a set deadline for a fixed price.
6. A famous experiment of the 1970s that highlights the principle that researchers should protect people being studied from possible physical or psychological harm. In the study the researcher created prison-like conditions and assigned <u>subjects</u> to play the role of guards or prisoners. The experiment ended early because of the violent realism of <u>subject</u> behavior.
7. A famous <u>field research</u> study that highlighted <u>anonymity</u> and <u>confidentiality</u>. The researcher covertly observed sexual contact among male homosexuals in a public restroom. Later he located their home and interviewed them in a disguise.
8. The ethical protection for those who are studied of holding research data in confidence or keeping them secret from the public; not releasing information in a way that permits

linking specific individuals to specific responses. Researchers do this by only presenting data in an aggregate form (e.g., percentages, means, etc.).

9. The ethical protection that the people studied remain nameless; their identity is protected from disclosure and remains unknown.

10. A famous experiment that highlighted the issue of protecting <u>subjects</u> from psychological harm. In the study the experimenter instructed <u>subjects</u> to administer increasingly intense electric shocks to another person for failing to learn. Many <u>subjects</u> became upset and falsely believed that they had caused severe physical harm to an innocent person.

11. A study in the 1950s that highlights violation of the <u>principle of voluntary consent,</u> a lack of <u>informed consent,</u> and government interference in social research. In the study researchers tape recorded jury deliberations without consent from jury members. Afterwards a law was passed that prohibited research on juries.

12. A controversial research project funded by the U.S. army in the 1960's that highlights a violation of the <u>principle of voluntary consent</u> and of a principle to show respect for people in a host country in comparative research. In the study American researchers secretly studied political protest by peasants and the poor in Chile.

13. A list of principles and guidelines by offered by professional organizations to guide research practice and clarify behaviors that are ethical.

14. A committee at U.S. colleges, hospitals, and research institutes that is required by federal law to ensure that research involving humans is conducted in a responsible, ethical manner.

15. an idea proposed by Karl Mannheim that professional academic researchers and free intellectuals occupy a unique social position. They are detached from the major groups in society which puts them in the best position to develop unbiased knowledge about all social groups and issues.

16. When someone engages in <u>research fraud</u>, <u>plagiarism,</u> or other unethical conduct that significantly deviates from the accepted practice for conducting and reporting research within the <u>scientific community</u>.

17. A set of <u>ideal type</u> ways that social researchers understand the purpose for conducting research and the proper use of research results.

18. A type of unethical behavior in which one uses another's writings or ideas without giving proper credit; "stealing ideas."

19. An international code of what constitutes moral, ethical behavior that was the beginning of <u>codes of ethics</u> for human research. It was adopted after the war crime trials of World War II in response to inhumane Nazi medical experiments.

20. An ethical principle that people should never participate in research unless they first explicitly agree to do so.

21. The ideal that science must be totally objective and based on empirical evidence alone. There is no place for a culture's values or a researcher's personal values or beliefs.

22. A type of <u>experimental design</u> in which all groups receive the <u>treatment</u> so that discomfort or benefits are shared and inequality is not created.

NAME _____ **DATE** _____

MATCHING KEY TERMS FOR CHAPTER 5

____	Academic Freedom	____	Nuremberg Code
____	Anonymity	____	Plagiarism
____	Bad Blood	____	Principle of Voluntary Consent

___	Code of Ethics	___	Project Camelot
___	Confidentiality	___	Relational Position
___	Contract Research	___	Research Fraud
___	Crossover Design	___	Scientific Misconduct
___	Informed Consent	___	Tearoom Trade Study
___	Institutional Review Board (IRB)	___	Wichita Jury Study
___	Milgram's Obedience Study	___	Value Neutrality
___	Models of Relevance	___	Zimbardo Prison Experiment

Exercise 5.1

Locate three articles from scholarly social work journals published in the past five years. Select one that uses survey research, one that is field research, and one that is an experiment. Determine the "model of relevance" that the author(s) implicitly accept. Attach a photocopy of the three articles and answer the following questions on each.

(1) What model was used and what helped you to identify the model of relevance?

(2) What ethical principles (e.g., confidentiality, debriefing, deception) regarding human subjects, if any, did the article discuss?

Survey

Field

Experiment

Exercise 5.2

Find out about your college's or university IRB. If it does not have one, ask your teacher to explain why it does not. If it does, find out who the members are and ask to attend a meeting as an observer when a "non-exempt" social research project is being discussed. Obtain a copy of the informed consent form used and write a short description of the meeting and issues discussed at it.

Exercise 5.3

Locate a college teacher in a department outside the social work (e.g., English, History, Math), and someone who is in administration (e.g., a dean, assistant dean, etc.). Interview each about the meaning of "academic freedom." Look up the term in an unabridged dictionary. Do you find different meanings of the term? Write a three-page essay explaining what you found.

Exercise 5.4

Role play the following situation on videotape or live before the class. Mr. or Ms. X has worked for the Department of Social Services (DSS) for six months conducting social work research. X thinks s/he is doing a good job and has a chance to build a satisfying, secure career at DSS. This is important to X because such jobs are difficult to come by. One day, Mr. Z, who is X's supervisor, comes into X's office and closes the door. In a serious tone, Mr. Z asks X to "adjust" the sampling frame and change five questions in a survey that will be conducted by DSS about recent welfare reform initiatives. The original sampling frame included country offices all across the state, but Mr. Z wants to drop seven areas where few minorities live. Mr. Z wants the questions on the questionnaire modified to increase estimates of people leaving welfare and show a gain in families that are becoming self-sufficient. Mr. Z said that this will make the central DSS office look much better. Strong results will help DSS get future funding. Mr. Z says that DSS regularly gets large appropriates from the State Budget Office and he does not want to lose access to additional resources. He also says all state welfare offices do this type of modification, and no one will get hurt. There is a hidden threat in the request: X's future career at DSS depends on X being a "team player" who understands the needs of the agency. Also, if funding is cut, X will be first on the layoff list. If X proves to be a loyal employee who does what s/he is told on this important request, his/her future at DSS looks much better. The only problem is that Mr. Z's request is unethical.

Exercise 5.5

Locate a copy of the Code of Ethics for a social science association in the U.S. or another country that involves human subjects. Some examples include the American Anthropological Association, American Political Science Association, American Psychological Association, Public Opinion Research Association, and so forth. You may have to search the Internet for the organization's homepage, or ask a college teacher in that academic field or a reference library for assistance.

Compare the NASW Code of Ethics in the textbook Appendix with the new one. Attach a copy of the new code of ethics and write a two-page essay discussing the similarities and differences between the new one and that of NASW.

Exercise 5.6

Visit at least three web sites selected from the list of Ethics and Human Subjects Issues sites in Chapter 5. Explore the selected sites looking for material that might be on interest to social workers or human services settings. In one or two paragraphs describe what you found in each of your three sites. Describe any links to other sites and indicate in general whether these links seem to involve social work content or whether they discuss matters that would be of interest in a human services setting. Tell whether you would recommend these to a colleague interested in the type of content covered in each site.

PRACTICE QUIZ 2, Chapters 4-5 (14 questions)

1. **Verstehen** basically means
    a. Voluntarism   d. Understanding
    b. Reification   e. Relativism
    c. Inductive

    USE FOR 2 TO 4:
    a. Positivism   b. Interpretative Social Science   c. Critical Social Science

2. Dr. Smith said that social science has to be value neutral, and a good study requires replication so that the laws of society can be discovered. Which approach to social science does she use?

3. Dr. Garcia says that the purpose of research is to smash myths and empower people. Which approach does he use?

4. Dr. Dubois want her theory to be grounded in people's lives and read like a novel. Which approach does she use?

5. What does the **Positivist** view say about free will and human nature?
    a. People can make choices and control their destiny, because they have partial autonomy. People have choices within constraints or structures. If they become aware of the constraints and collectively try to change the constraints, they can create a better world.
    b. Free will is a fiction; it is a term which describes areas of human behavior for which we have not yet discovered the causal laws of human society.
    c. Human behavior is not determined by fixed laws. Rather, people actively create their social realities in an on-going process. Human behavior is based upon social interactions and personal reasons which are based on interpretations of events using a meaning system.
    d. What a person does is explained by systematically documenting the external forces or laws acting upon him/her. Social scientists may not be able to exactly predict what a specific person will do can state the precise probability of a person doing something based on causal factors.
    e. b and d

6. Professor Davis's results will be reported where most scientific research first appears. Where is this?
    a. Television news   d. Scholarly journals
    b. Newspapers   e. College textbooks
    c. Newsmagazines

7. According to **Critical Social Science** humans are fundamentally:
    a. Beings who create meaning and try to make sense of their world.
    b. Creative beings with great potential who are trapped by illusion and exploitation.
    c. Self-interested and rational beings shaped by outside forces.
    d. Beings with little free will whose actions are predictable.
    e. Beings who act on the basis of motives, reasons and personal feelings.

8. Which of the five models of relevance fits the following quotation?

   We find that the same social conditions and behaviors are defined by some as a social problem and by others as agreeable. Yet, there is a core of conditions which nearly everyone holds to be undesirable (crime, poverty, epidemics). Sociological truth may not instantly make us free of the problems or eliminate dysfunctions in society. But by discovering the consequences of actual practices and making these known, sociology provides a basis for their reexamination and perhaps, in the long run, their modification.

   a. Special Constituency-The Proletariat   d. Special Constituency-The Uncoopted
   b. Direct and Positive Effects   e. Special Constituency-Government Officials
   c. No Net Effects

9. Which of the following would **NOT** be considered as a "special population" for social research purposes?

   a. A group of eight-year old children.   d. A random sample of adults at a shopping mall.
   b. The prisoners at a state prison.   e. Students in an introduction to social work class.
   c. Homeless people at a shelter.

10. Which is the principle of ethics most likely to have been seriously violated in the situation described below?

   People who go to a drug treatment center to get help for heroin addiction are told that they can volunteer to become subjects in a study on a new treatment, but they will not be told whether they are in the control or experimental group. The volunteers are randomly divided into two groups. One group of volunteers receives a placebo (no drug at all) and the other group receives a drug which previous research has shown to be highly effective in reducing heroin dependency. After two years in the study, the researcher compares the two groups for heroin dependency.

   a. Do not cause physical harm to subjects
   b. Do not create unnecessary psychological stress or anxiety
   c. Do not place subject in legal jeopardy
   d. Protect the confidentiality of subjects
   e. Do not create new inequalities

11. We can learn about ethics based "famous cases." Which study is the "famous case" in which college students were used in a very life-like experiment. Unexpectedly, the subjects became highly involved in the roles of the experiment. Realizing that the subjects had lost perspective and forgot they were in an experiment and fearing they could be harmed, the researcher ended the experiment one week early. The principle to protect the subjects from harm took precedence over the need to complete the experiment.

   a. Tearoom Trade   d. Zimbardo Prison Experiment
   b. Project Camelot   e. Bad Blood
   c. Milgram Obedience Experiment

12. Survey researcher, Slim Slime, telephones respondents and lies by telling them he is from "University Opinion Research." He gives no other identifying information; he does not tell them that the survey is voluntary or what it is about, but immediately asks personal questions. The respondents never learn who Mr. Slime really was. Afterwards, Mr. Slime gives a market research company each respondent's name and address attached to their answers to questions. What ethical principle(s) has he violated?

a. Failing to get informed consent
b. Breach of confidentiality
c. Inappropriate use of deception
d. All of the above
e. None of the above; this is standard practice and is ethical.

13.   An <u>informed consent statement</u> would **NOT** include:
   a. How much money it costs the researcher to conduct the study
   b. A guarantee of anonymity and confidentiality
   c. A description of the procedure of the study
   d. A statement that participation is completely voluntary
   e. All are included

14.   An official at a government agency visits a social researcher and tells the researcher to stop an on-going study on the social consequences of industrial pollution. The official says that the study should be stopped because it might upset public opinion, disturb important community leaders, and increase discontent with government policy. If the researcher refuses to end the study, the government official implies that the researcher might lose his job at the university and not be able to get any future research funding. This illustrates what ethical-political problem?

   a. Scientific misconduct occurred
   b. Research fraud occurred
   c. Academic freedom was violated
   d. Plagiarism occurred
   e. There was a lack of objectivity by the researcher

QUALITATIVE AND QUANTITATIVE RESEARCH DESIGNS

LEARNING OBJECTIVES

After studying Chapter 6 you will be able to do the following:
1. Understand variables and be able to identify independent, dependent, and intervening variables;
2. Understand the three requirements for a causal relationship;
3. Identify and create a hypothesis that contains the five characteristics of causal hypotheses;
4. Understand the *logic of the disconfirming hypothesis* and its relation to the *null hypothesis*;
5. Identify a *double-barreled hypothesis* and know why it should be avoided;
6. Read causal diagrams with up to five variables and take a hypothesis with at least three variables and draw a causal diagram for it;
7. Understand *units of analysis* and be able to apply the idea in specific situations;
8. Recognize the *ecological fallacy, reductionism, tautology, teleology* and *spuriousness* in a specific situation and understand why they are not good causal hypotheses;
9. Take a general topic and narrow it down into a highly specific research question and hypothesis, stating the variables and direction of causality;
10. Identify the topic, research question, major hypothesis, variables, unit of analysis and the universe in a less-complex scholarly journal article.

MATCHING DEFINITIONS

1. A statement that appears to be a <u>causal explanation</u>, but is not because the <u>dependent variable</u> is really only a restatement of the <u>independent variable</u>; it is true "by definition."
2. The kind of <u>empirical</u> case or unit that a researcher observes, measures and analyzes in a study.
3. The categories or levels of a variable.
4. The first variable that causes or produces the effect in a <u>causal explanation</u>.
5. A variable that is between the initial causal variable and the final effect variable in a <u>causal explanation</u>.
6. The broad class of units that are covered in a <u>hypothesis.</u> All the units to which the findings of a specific study might be generalized.
7. A statement that appears to be a <u>causal explanation</u>, but is not because a hidden, unmeasured or initially unseen variable. The unseen variable comes earlier in the <u>temporal order,</u> and it has a causal impact on the what was initially posited to be the <u>independent</u> variable as well as the <u>dependent variable</u>.
8. A way to talk about the scope of a <u>social theory, causal explanation, proposition, hypothesis</u> or theoretical statement. The range of phenomena it covers or to which it applies, from social psychological, <u>micro-level</u>, to organizational, <u>meso-level</u>, to large-scale social structure, <u>macro-level</u>.
9. A <u>hypothesis</u> that says there is no relationship or <u>association</u> between two variables, or no effect.

10. The effect variable that is last and results from the causal variable(s) in a causal explanation. Also the variable that is measured in the pretest and posttest, and that is the result of the treatment in experimental research.
11. A rare test of two or more competing explanations of the same phenomenon. The test results will clearly show that one social theory is correct and the other(s) is(are) false.
12. Something that appears to be a causal explanation, but is not. It occurs because of a confusion about units of analysis. A researcher has empirical evidence about an association for large-scale units or huge aggregates, but overgeneralizes to make theoretical statements about an association among small-scale units or individuals.
13. Something that appears to be a causal explanation, but is not because of a confusion about units of analysis. A researcher has empirical evidence for an association at the level of individual behavior or very small-scale units, but overgeneralizes to make theoretical statements about very large-scale units.
14. The basis of the null hypothesis. It is the idea that it is easier to find empirical evidence that supports an association than against it. It means that when testing a causal explanation, researchers try to find evidence that fails to support an association, and not just for evidence that supports it.
15. The statement from a causal explanation or a proposition that has at least one independent and one dependent variable, but it has yet to be empirically tested.
16. A hypothesis that has more than one independent variable and is stated in a confusing way that makes it unclear whether each independent variable separately has an effect or only the combination of both together affects the dependent variable.
17. A hypothesis paired with a null hypothesis stating that the independent variable has an effect on a dependent variable.
18. A statement that appears to be a causal explanation, but is not because it cannot be tested empirically. The independent variable is an amorphous idea, a long-term goal, future intention or characteristic of an entire system. It usually lacks a clear temporal order prior to the dependent variable.
19. A type of concept or construct, or the empirical indicator of a construct, that takes on two or more levels or values.
20. A characteristic of the qualitative style in which a researcher creatively works with his/her hands and pragmatically combined diverse odds and ends to accomplish a specific task.
21. Social theory that is rooted in observations of specific, concrete details.
22. A term borrowed from surveying the land that says looking at an object from several different points gives a more accurate view of it.
23. An orientation toward social research in which the researcher accepts with little or no question the research questions as government officials, corporate leaders or bureaucratic superiors formulate them. The researcher then conducts studies, often applied research, that will provide the officials with information to help them make decisions in a bureaucratic organization.
24. An orientation towards research in which the researcher develops research questions based on independent judgement or the concerns of the people being studied. The researcher moves beyond current arrangements and tries to assist the people being studied gain greater understanding and control over their lives.
25. A logic of doing research based on reorganizing the practices and ideas for doing good research into a set of coherent, systematic, formal rules and techniques. Researchers standardize the rules and techniques, codify them in textbooks, and teach them by formal instruction. It is used more often in the quantitative research style.
26. A logic of doing social research based on having informal discussions among active researchers about how to do social research. It grows from how the researchers addressed

practical problems in specific studies they conducted, it is taught largely by an apprenticeship method, and it most used in a qualitative style of research.

27. Research that proceeds in a clear, logical, step-by-step straight line. It is more characteristic of a quantitative than a qualitative approach to social research.

28. Research that proceeds in a circular, back-and-forth manner. It is more characteristic of a qualitative than a quantitative style to social research.

29. In qualitative research, what the people who are being studied actually feel and think.

30. In qualitative research, what a researcher believes the people being studied feel and think.

31. In qualitative research, what a researcher tells the reader of a research report that the people he or she studied felt and thought.

NAME _____ DATE

MATCHING TERMS FOR CHAPTER 6

___ Alternate Hypothesis   ___ Non-Linear Research Path
___ Attributes   ___ Null Hypothesis
___ Bricolage   ___ Reconstructed Logic
___ Crucial Experiment   ___ Reductionism
___ Dependent Variable   ___ Second Order Interpretation
___ Double-Barrelled Hypothesis   ___ Spuriousness
___ Ecological Fallacy   ___ Tautology
___ First Order Interpretation   ___ Technocratic Perspective
___ Grounded Theory   ___ Teleology
___ Hypothesis   ___ Third-Order Interpretation
___ Independent Variable   ___ Transcendent Perspective
___ Intervening Variable   ___ Triangulation
___ Level of Analysis   ___ Unit of Analysis
___ Linear Research Path   ___ Universe
___ Logic in Practice   ___ Variable
___ Logic of Disconfirming Hypotheses

Exercise 6.1

Part 1: The six case studies below has each of the following five problems and one has nothing wrong with it: **Ecological Fallacy, Reductionism, Spuriousness, Tautology, Teleology, or Nothing wrong.** Match the problem (or nothing wrong) to the appropriate case. Put X in the box below.

Part 2: For each of the six cases identify the **independent and dependent variable**.

	CASE 1 Rubber Glove	CASE 2 Little Donkey	CASE 3 Prison Construc- tion	CASE 4 DWI	CASE 5 Abused Children	CASE 6 Urban Blight
Ecological Fallacy						
Reductionism						
Spuriousness						
Tautology						
Teleology						
Nothing Wrong						
INDEPEND- ENT VARIABLE						
DEPEND- ENT VARIABLE						

CASE 1: BIG RUBBER GLOVES, CO.

In 2001, the Vice President for Human Resource of Big Rubber Gloves, Inc. developed a new day care program for employees. He asked Assistant Manager Mary Smithkowski to evaluate how employees felt about the day care program and their level of satisfaction with it. To do her research Mary went to the administration department of Big Rubber Gloves where she gathered information on each of the company's 100 plants in various world-wide locations. For each plant she gathered information on the cost of the program per week and the average weekly productivity and absentee rates. Mary found that the program cost was over $150,000 a year at 40 plants. At these plants the absentee rate was 15 percent per week and productivity was 600 gloves per worker per week. At another 40 plants, the program cost was $100,000 or less per year. For the low cost plants the absentee rate was 20 percent and production was 400 gloves per week. The remaining 20 plants had program costs of between $100,000 and $150,000 per year, and an absentee rate of 16 per cent and a production rate of 500 gloves per week.

Mary reasoned that high cost day care programs produced low absentee rates and high productivity rates. Plants with low a program cost also had a low absentee rate, but a lower productivity rate. Mary's report concluded that the employees found the day care program valuable and were highly satisfied with it. She recommended continuing the program because so many employees who used the program were productive, happy workers.

CASE 2: LITTLE DONKEY ELEMENTARY SCHOOL

Pablo Pollino is the principal of the Little Donkey Elementary School. He wants to find out why the Latino students in his school have much lower achievement scores than students with an Asian, African, or Anglo heritage. He is concerned because one-fourth of the students are Latino. Their scores have been the lowest of all groups for the past two years. He reasoned that if he can identify the cause of the difference, he might be able to assist the students. He felt that the people who work with the students on a daily basis, teachers, will be a good source of information.

Mr. Pollino sends a questionnaire to all the school's teachers. It asks "Why have Latino children scored the worst?" He was happy that 155 of the 160 teachers returned the questionnaire in ten days. All but two wrote the same thing, "Society does not want them to succeed." Pablo noted this high level of agreement. He says that he now knows that there is nothing he can do to raise the achievement scores of Latino children. Society does not want it, and he cannot control society.

CASE 3: GROWTH IN PRISON CONSTRUCTION

Professor Chen Lo decided to study state prison construction in the United States. He examined the pattern of construction of new prisons and the expansion of existing prisons during the past two decades. He found that there was a dramatic growth during the period, 1980-2000. Professor Lo investigated the factors associated with prison construction. Examining the many factors associated with prison construction he came across one which seemed to be critical -- spending funds for prison construction by state government agencies. He found that whenever state government spent more money to build or expand prisons, more state prisons were built or expanded. In fact, he did not find a single exception where increased spending for prison construction was not followed by more prisons. In his conclusion, Professor Lo stated that the large increase in new and expanded prisons was caused by spending money for prison construction. If people wanted to control the growth and expansion of prisons, they should stop spending money for that purpose.

CASE 4: DWI IN WOODSBORO

Probation officer Henri Lefevbre of Woodsboro, Ontario conducted research for his MSW degree. He studied the problem of DWI in Canada by looking at arrest records of various police agencies and traveling with intoxicated driver police patrols. He interviewed other police and probation officers and examined statistics. After a year of research, the officer thought he uncovered the reason for driving while intoxicated.

Officer Lefevbre discovered that a majority of the people that the police had arrested for driving while intoxicated had a particular personality type. They were high risk-takers. These people took risks in other areas of their lives. He confirmed this hypothesis by interviewing 1,000 people in three provinces between the ages of 18 and 40 who had been arrested for DWI. He also conducted interviews with 1,000 similar people who police had never arrested for DWI. He found that those who police had arrested for DWI were much more likely to have a risk-taking personality as measured by two standardized clinical scales. These people got a sense of excitement or a thrill from experiencing high risk, and they blocked thinking about negative consequences. Such people were more likely to engage in other high risk behaviors (e.g., enjoy high risk sports, never wear seat belts, gamble, smoke, etc.), than those who police had never arrested for DWI. Thus, he found that some people have a personality that makes them less sensitive to something bad happening because of their behavior. These are the people who are more likely to drink and drive.

As a further check the probation officer asked all 2,000 people whether they thought driving after drinking was risky behavior. He found that 85 percent of both groups agreed that drinking then driving was risky. The risk-taking people were not as worried that something (e.g., arrest, an accident) would happen to them. People with a particular type of personality were more willing to take a chance, because they felt a need for excitement and felt lucky.

CASE 5: ABUSED CHILDREN

Cindy Running Bear studied battered women for her senior honor's thesis in social work. She wanted to explain why unmarried women who lived with their children abused them. She went to the library and read extensively on the topic. Cindy discovered that unmarried women with children were more likely to smoke cigarettes and watch violent TV shows than the general population. She also found that the women who abused their children were more likely to have grown up in homes in which they had been abused when children. Research studies she read suggested that abused children are more likely to smoke cigarettes when they become adults. In addition, abused children are more likely to be attracted to television, especially action-oriented, violent shows, as a method of escape. She also read that people who had been abused as children are more likely to become abusers as adults. This is because they learned it as a model of adult-child behavior. After summarizing the literature, Cindy concluded that the cause of unmarried women abusing their children was their television watching and smoking habits. She thought that this self-destructive and escapist behavior promoted the abuse of children. She reasoned that if social workers could encourage the unmarried women to watch less television and stop smoking, then the problem of abused children would end.

CASE 6: URBAN BLIGHT

Dr. Susan Bedford studied the development of urban blight in major British cities between 1966 and 1999. She noticed that center city districts of most major cities had population decline. The number of city people unemployed rose. At the same time poverty, pollution, crime, and congestion increased. During the decades center city areas developed blocks of abandoned buildings, taxes increased and fewer businesses invested money for expansion. In addition, traffic congestion grew as cities mushroomed.

During her investigation Dr. Bedford discovered a little known government bureaucrat in the Department of Red Tape, Confusion and Mismanagement, Harvey Wakeup. Mr. Wakeup had been assigned the task of preparing a national program on urban blight in 1968. Unfortunately, Mr. Wakeup had serious personal problems and went on medical leave for 26 years. During his absence, no one else was assigned to his task. In 1996, two years after he returned to work, he became confused one day and accidentally hit a button that destroyed all his work that had been stored in a computer. In frustration, Mr. Wakeup retired from work the next day.

Dr. Bedford saw that due to circumstances involving Mr. Wakeup, the British government failed to develop a response to the problem of urban blight. Dr. Bedford concluded that the cause of British urban blight was the misfortune of Harvey Wakeup. If only Harvey had done his job, the problem of urban blight would not be with us today.

Exercise 6.2

Identify the Unit of Analysis, Universe and Dependent Variable in each of the seven condensed summaries of articles below. You may wish to go to the library and read them, but there is sufficient information here.

Janet Gornick and Jerry Jacobs in "Gender, the Welfare State and Public Employment" *American Sociological Review, 63*, 688-710 (1998) examined the impact of public employment on the gap between private and public sector wages and on the gap between male and female wages in seven advanced industrial nations. Data on variables for each nation came from the Luxemburg Income Study for the year 1989-1992. The size of the public sector varies greatly by country, from 41.5

percent of all working adults in Sweden to 17.1 in the United States. The authors found that nations with a large public sector, pay for government employment is almost equal to that of the private sector, but in nations with a smaller public sector employment, government pay is higher. They did not find a consistent effect of public sector size on the gender pay gap.

In "Labor Markets, Industrial Monopolization, Welfare and Imprisonment: Evidence from a Cross-Section of U.S. Counties." *Sociological Quarterly, 31*, 41-458 (1990) Mark Colvin examined whether the rate of unemployment was related to rates of welfare, and how unemployment and welfare affected rates of imprisonment. He gathered data from a random sample of 184 urban, industrial counties in the United States. For each county he measured many variables including: unemployment rate, liberalism of government, percentage of county population below the poverty line, welfare payments per recipient, crime rate, and the rate per 100,000 county population of new commitments to state penal facilities.

In "The Impact of Distance Education Programs on Community Agencies." *Research on Social Work Practice*, 10(4), 438-453 (2000) Jo Ann McFall and Paul Freddolino examined the impacts of distance education programs on clients, field instructors, cooperating agencies, and the networks of agencies that surround these distance education sites. Previous research on distance education programs concluded that the presence of MSW students tended to encourage agencies in which the students were placed to support the special needs populations of the community. The authors conducted interviews on sets of focus groups in order to better understand the issues that impacted the distant agencies. Surveys were mailed with return postage paid to the agency directors, field instructors, and students participating in the distance education programs. Response rates ranged from 37.5% for students to 55.6% for field instructors. There were a total of 266 surveys returned from the 362 originally sent. Data from the surveys was entered into SPSS for analysis. It was found that the presence of students in the distant agencies increased services provided to special needs clients and also increased new programs. The authors concluded that distance education programs had reached the goals of providing a quality education to students across the state, while improving the community's resources.

In "Self-Perceptions of Black Americans: Self-Esteem and Personal Efficacy" *American Journal of Sociology, 95*, 132-159 (1989) Michael Hughes and David Demo examined two kinds of self-esteem: personal self esteem (an individual's belief in his or her own virtue and moral worth), and efficacy (a sense of competence or personal control). Curious about a finding in past studies that black Americans showed high personal self-esteem but low efficacy, the authors looked at data from the National Survey of Black Americans. It is a sample of 2,107 black individuals, 18 years old and older who were interviewed in 1979 or 1980. Information on many variables was gathered: years of education, occupation, employment, job characteristics, family relations, friendships, attitudes towards self, attitudes about personal power, beliefs about black people as a group, etc.

In "Validating School Social Work: An Evaluation of a Cognitive-Behavioral Approach to Reduce School Violence." *Research on Social Work Practice, 9*(4), 399-426 (1999) Gary Whitfield wanted to learn whether cognitive behavioral methods of anger management had a significant affect on school violence. He posed three questions: (1) how effective was social work in using cognitive-behavioral methods to reduce school violence? (2) When trying to improve anger control, is a specific or general approach more effective? (3) Are anger control gains still apparent in subjects after six months? He obtained sixteen subjects from his existing caseload of adolescent boys in the school. He assigned members of the pairs of boys to either the control or the experimental group. The control group did not receive any extra skills training beyond what they would have originally under the author's caseload. The experimental group, in addition to the typical social work treatment, also received skills training in relaxation techniques, anger reducers, thought-stopping techniques and problem-solving skills. The author found that students who had participated in the Anger Control training had generally positive changes. They had fewer behavioral problems than subjects not receiving the training, as well as more positive expressions of anger. The author is quick to point out, however, that with such a small sample there were many outside influencing factors that the study could not control for.

In "Psychosocial and spiritual care in hospice: Differences between nursing, social work, and clergy." *The Hospice Journal, 12*(1), 29-41 (1997) Dona Reese and Dean Brown studied the extent to which the hospice environment attended to the psychosocial and spiritual needs of their clients, and which of the staff members so engaged. A traditional hospice framework focuses on issues in a holistic fashion, but psychosocial and spiritual concerns are often viewed as secondary and the nursing staff usually addresses them. This study examined visits recorded on the charts of 36 hospice patients, analyzing the documentation of specific psychosocial and spiritual issues discussed during the visits. The types of issues discussed and recorded for each visit included denial, anxiety about death, hospice values, social support, and spirituality. The researchers analyzed the frequency with which the various types of issues were discussed and which staff position discussed it. Patient length of stay in the hospice was also recorded and found to be significant in the frequency of the discussion topics. Results showed that nurses discussed hospice values and denial most frequently, social workers were more likely to discuss anxiety about death and social support, and clergy most often addressed spirituality issues. The frequency of issues discussed in this study does reflect the hospice as a holistic setting, although the authors contend that there should be more emphasis placed in the psychosocial and spiritual aspects of patients.

In "Strikebreaking or solidarity in the Great Steel Strike of 1919: A split labor market, game-theoretic and QCA analysis" in *American Journal of Sociology*, *100*, 1479-1519 (1995) Cliff Brown and Terry Boswell tried to explain whether black and white workers joined together in labor disputes. They collected data on 16 Northern U.S. cities that had labor disputes during a wave of labor strikes in steel industry in 1919. They sought to explain the degree of solidarity among black and white workers during the strikes. They considered the strength of the union in prior disputes, whether local politics were pro- or anti-union, city size, and how recently black workers had migrated to the Northern city from the South.

Authors of Article	Unit of Analysis	Universe	Dependent Variable
Gornick and Jacobs			
Colvin			
McFall and Freddolino			
Hughes and Demo			
Whitfield			
Reese and Brown			
Brown and Boswell			

Exercise 6.3

Draw a causal diagram of the three quantitative studies discussed in the textbook, you may want to look up and read the full article:
1. **EXPERIMENT**: Neapolitan "The Effects of Different Types of Praise and Criticism on Performance"
2. **SURVEY RESEARCH**: Bankston and Thompson "Carrying Firearms for Protection"
3. **CONTENT ANALYSIS**: Barlow, Barlow & Chiricos "Economic Conditions and Ideologies of Crime in the Media"

Exercise 6.4
Locate the following scholarly journal article: Becker, Penny Edgell (1998) "Making Inclusive Communities: Congregations and the 'Problem' of Race." *Social Problems, 45,* 451-72. Identify evidence in the article that illustrates three of the four following concepts: (1) Bricolage (2) First, Second and Third Order Interpretations (3) Transcendent Perspective (4) Grounded Theory.

CHAPTER 7

QUALITATIVE AND QUANTITATIVE MEASUREMENT

LEARNING OBJECTIVES

After studying Chapter 7 you will be able to do the following:
1. Describe the measurement process and how to move from an abstract construct to a specific indicator;
2. Explain the role of conceptualization and operationalization, and develop conceptual and operational definitions for variables.
3. Contrast quantitative and qualitative approaches to conceptualization and operationization;
4. Define the idea of reliability, specify the three types of reliability and explain how to check for and improve each type.
5. Define measurement validity, distinguish it from other types of validity,;
6. Explain how conceptual and empirical hypothesis differ.
7. Explain four major types of measurement validity and subtypes with them;
8. Discuss the four levels of measurement, differences among them, and identify the level of a specific indicator;
9. Understand the purpose and uses of standardization, indexes and scaling in social measurement;
10. Explain how unidimensionality and mutually exclusive and exhaustive categories are used in scale and index construction.

MATCHING DEFINITIONS
1. How well an empirical indicator and the conceptual definition of the construct that the indicator is supposed to measure "fit" together.
2. The dependability or consistency of the measure of a variable.
3. A "law" used in Thurstone scaling that says if many people independently compare and rank a set of items, researchers can treat the items on which most people subjectively agree and give a similar rank as being at an interval-level of measurement.
4. The procedure to statistically adjust measures to permit making an honest comparison by giving a common basis to measures of different units.
5. A type of measurement validity in which an indicator "makes sense" as a measure of a construct in the judgement of others, especially those in the scientific community.
6. Rules that researchers use to reduce the gap between the abstract constructs and specific measurement operations they use in concrete social reality.
7. A supplemental theory that researchers use to reduce the gap between the abstract constructs and specific measurement operations they use.
8. The process developing a clear, rigorous, systematic conceptual definitions for abstract ideas/concepts.
9. The process of moving from the conceptual definition of a construct to a set of specific activities or measures that allow a researcher to observe it empirically, i.e. its operational definition.
10. A type of hypothesis in which the researcher expresses variables in abstract, conceptual terms and expresses the relationship among variables in a theoretical way.
11. A type of hypothesis in which the researcher expresses variables in specific empirical terms and expresses the association among the measured indicators in observable, empirical terms.

____	Content Validity	____	Ordinal-Level Measurement
____	Continuous Variables	____	Predictive Validity
____	Convergent Validity	____	Ratio-Level Measurement
____	Criterion Validity	____	Reliability
____	Discrete Variables	____	Representative Reliability
____	Discriminant Validity	____	Rules of Correspondence
____	Empirical Hypothesis	____	Scale
____	Equivalence Reliability	____	Semantic Differential
____	Exhaustive Attributes	____	Split-Half Method
____	External Validity	____	Stability Reliability
____	Face Validity	____	Standardization
____	Guttman Scale	____	Statistical Validity
____	Index	____	Subpopulation Analysis
____	Intercoder Reliability	____	Test-Retest Method
____	Internal Validity	____	Thurstone Scaling
____	Interval-Level Measurement	____	Unidimensionality
____	Law of Comparative Judgement	____	Validity
____	Levels of Measurement		

Exercise 7.1

Suppose you want to test the following hypothesis: Caseworkers who have more training have less burnout.

1. Develop a <u>conceptual definition</u> for training.

2. Develop a <u>conceptual definition</u> for burnout.

3. Assume you operationalize the independent variable as a Caseworker's number of in-service workshops attended. What validity problems does this create?

4. Develop an <u>operational definition</u> of the dependent variable at an <u>ordinal level of measurement</u>.

5. State your <u>empirical hypothesis</u>:

6. Explain how you might test the <u>reliability</u> of your dependent variable measure.

Exercise 7.2

Go to the library locate a research-oriented article from one of the following scholarly journals:. <u>International Social Work</u>, <u>Journal of Social Service Research</u>, <u>Journal of Sociology and Social Welfare</u>, <u>Social Work</u>, <u>Social Service Review</u>, or <u>Social Work Abstracts</u>. Attach a photocopy of the article.

1. What is the **topic** of the article?

2. What is the main conceptual **hypothesis** being tested in the article?

3. How is the **dependent variable** defined conceptually?

4. How is the **dependent variable** measured?

5. Discuss the **reliability** (any type) of the **dependent variable.**

6. Discuss the **validity** (any type) of the **dependent variable.**

7. What is a different way to measure the same **dependent variable**?

Exercise 7.3

Professor Peavely conducted a study on 150 social work students in 3 sections of Practice Skills. She wanted to improve student learning and test a learning theory she picked up from Hank Hardnose's Dog Obedience School. He thought that dogs and students learn the most when they are highly motivated and that threats lead to greater motivation for students or dogs. She gave a speech in Section 1 of Practice Skills on the first class day in a stern, serious tone. She emphasized that this was a very hard course. She said students would fail unless they got at least 80 percent correct on a difficult comprehensive final exam. In Section 2 she omitted the statement about the course difficulty. She used a less stern tone and said the cutoff for F's was 60 percent. In Section 3 she smiled and said this was an easy course. She stated that students only needed to get 30 percent on the final examination to pass the course. She measured motivation as the number of hours per week a student spent working in the video lab practicing their interviewing skills. She assumed that high motivation was indicated by spending at least 8 hours per week in the lab. She measured learning with the final exam score. She hoped to find that Section 1 students were more likely to spend at least 8 hours a week in the lab. In addition, that the students who spent at least 8 hours per week in the lab were more likely to get a higher score higher on the final examination than those who spent less than 8 hours per week.

1. What is the <u>independent variable</u> in general conceptual terms?

   The <u>intervening variable</u>?

   The <u>dependent variable</u>?

2. State the <u>conceptual hypothesis</u> of this study:

3. What is the <u>operational definition</u> of the <u>independent variable</u>?

   The <u>intervening variable</u>?

   The <u>dependent variable</u>?

4. State the <u>empirical hypothesis</u> of this study:

THE MUDTOWN NEWS

Read the above hypothetical newspaper article.

Our motto: All the mud that's fit to sling

Number of Teen Pregnancies Concern City Officials

The Mudtown Health Department released figures early this week on the number of pregnancies among high school girls at the city's high schools during 2001. At the East High School 60 girls became pregnant last year, at North High School 30 girls became pregnant, and at St. Ruth's High School 10 girls became pregnant last year. Sergeant John's Academy reports no pregnant girls among its students during 2001.

City Officials and social service agency officials state they are concerned about this serious problem. The mayor announced the creation of a Pregnancy Task Force to investigate the problem at East High School. Principal John Jones of North High School stated that he is concerned, but feels the problem is under control. He said, "The problem at North has not reached the epidemic situation with which East High School is plagued." He will continue to monitor the problem. Sister Sue of St. Ruth's stated, "The few pregnancies at our school demonstrates the importance of a religious-based education to instill a strong moral character." Sergeant John of Sergeant John's Academy said, "I would not expect a problem at our Academy. Our students have self-discipline. Our excellent record is due to our program of rigorous academic and physical training and high standards for all students."

After reading this article, you obtain the following 2001 enrollment statistics for each high school.

	East	North	St. Ruths	Sergeant John's
Boys	800	300	300	600
Girls	1200	600	200	8
Total	2000	900	500	608

Examine these enrollment statistics in light of the information offered in the news story. What can you say about the accuracy of this "news story?"

How does standardization help?

Exercise 7.5

(1) Identify the types of reliability or validity in each case below.
(2) Identify the type of scale or whether an index was used in each case below.

CASE 1: SAM'S USED CARS

Sam Slippery, a local used car dealer, developed a "SUCKER" measure for the student customer. He was able to size up a new customer and determine whether a college student would be someone who would pay an outrageous price for real junk. Sam's measure was based on assigning a "sucker number" to six features of a person then adding them up to get an overall score. For example, if the person wore mismatched plaids, they got a sucker number of 1 or 2 based on how bad the mismatch was. Sam said if anyone had a score of 10 or higher, he or she was a real sucker. Sam's sales staff knew they could unload a junker on the student. Sam checked how good his measure was by seeing whether or not he gave the same college student customer the same score when the customer came back a second or third time to look at cars. He found that once he rated a student as a sucker, the student stayed a sucker

CASE 2: HARRY THE THIEF

Harry Handsome is a jewel thief. He enters a store he is considering robbing and poses as a marketing representative. He asks the store manager to complete a short form on gem appreciation as the manager looks at a gem Harry holds. The form contains a set of extreme polar opposite adjectives and adverbs (e.g., hot/cold, slow/fast) with spaces between them. Harry asks the store manager to mark his overall feelings about the gem. Harry takes the form home and analyzes it. He has found that one pattern indicates good stores to rob, ones in which the managers are careless and do not feel good about high quality gems. In order to test his measure Harry had the recognized International Gem Institute give the same store managers a test on gems that has been used for years to measure gem knowledge. Harry found that his new test generally gives the same results as the one by the International Gem Institute, but his takes only half as long to complete.

CASE 3: BRENT AND PEOPLE WHO ARE HOMELESS

Brent Brillcream, a local concerned citizen, wants to measure attitudes towards individuals who are homeless. He first went out to look at some people in shelters and thought about the idea. Next, he developed 17 statements (e.g., most homeless people are psychiatrically disabled). He had five answer responses to each: Strongly Agree, Agree, No Opinion, Disagree, Strongly Disagree. Brent distributed his questions to 120 people. He checked his questions and discovered that young adults, 18-39 years old, tended to be honest and tell him their true attitudes with the 17 questions. For older people, 40-70 years old, he found that the questions did not elicit honest responses. The older people did not tell him their true attitude with the 17 questions and agreed with everything Brent said about people who were homeless no matter what he asked.

CASE 4: MARGE'S LIZARD

Marge Magpie is a pet lover. She wants to find out how people in her neighborhood feel about people who keep 3 meter-long human-eating lizards as house pets. First, she went door-to-door and asked 24 of her neighbors to answer a question. The question contained a list of statements, in order, regarding how close a person with a human-eating lizard was to the neighbor: in the same country, in the same town, in the same neighborhood, a next door neighbor, in the same apartment building, etc. She asked the neighbors to indicate at what point they felt uncomfortable. To determine how well her question measured the way people actually felt Marge went back to the same neighbors the next day. This time she took a rubber copy of a 3 meter-long human-eating lizard with her on a chain. When the neighbor opened the door, Marge tugged the chain, that was rigged to come apart suddenly. Marge shouted, "This is one of those human-eating lizards." She predicted that neighbors who expressed discomfort soonest on her question would be the first to scream, and they would do so louder than her other neighbors. In fact, she predicted that the neighbors who said that they felt comfortable with such a lizard in their apartment building or garden would not scream at all.

CASE 5: FELICE'S DOLLS

Felice Feltip has a huge doll collection and sells dolls. To help her evaluate her dolls she gathered together 25 friends and doll sellers. She attached a code number to each doll. She asked each of the 25 people to go into a room alone and judge each of the dolls one at a time. The judges rated each doll on a scale 1 to 9, where 1 mean "this is a plain, uninteresting, ordinary doll" and 9 mean"this is a special, interesting, unique doll." Felice took the results and calculated the amount of agreement among the judges and identifed the 10 dolls that most agreed to be special, the 10 the middle and the 10 least interesting and used this information to develop a pricing system in her store.

Exercise 7.6

STANDARDIZATION

State governments financially support public indigent families in the United States, but the level of public support varies greatly by state and changes over time. Below are hypothetical data from 18 states, their population, number of indigent families, and the amount of state publics money spent on income support for indigent families and the amount of money indigent families spend from their own (non-pubic) sources Numbers were rounded and adjusted so they are based on 1,000 to make calculations easier. Standardize the data to find true differences among the state support for indigent care families. **You should use a hand calculator for this exercise.**

State	Public Money in $1,000s	Indigent Family Money In $1,000s	State Population in 1,000s	Indigent Families in 1,000s
1. Alaska	155,800	38,800	609	17.4
2. Arizona	761,000	346,800	4,555	161.9
3. California	6,059,900	1,362,000	32,268	1,263.1
4. Colorado	482,300	432,500	3,893	136.1
5. Connecticut	428,700	192,800	3,270	57.0
6. Florida	1,660,500	509,800	14,654	403.0
7. Georgia	1,186,600	369,200	7,486	212.8
8. Hawaii	242,700	33,400	1,187	32.7
9. Illinois	1,844,900	459,600	11,896	353.2
10. Massachusetts	593,500	311,300	6,118	116.9
11. Mississippi	458,700	208,500	2,731	101.6
12. New York	2,226,700	1,080,900	18,137	439.3
13. Oklahoma	493,300	213,300	3,317	111.4
14. South Carolina	490,800	352,700	3,760	123.9
15. South Dakota	87,900	61,600	738	21.9
16. Vermont	36,700	132,600	589	15.3
17. Wisconsin	1,034,200	425,100	5,170	180.9
18. Wyoming	147,500	39,700	480	21.3

Exercise 7.6 continued

CALCULATE THE FOLLOWING FOR EACH STATE AND ANSWER THE QUESTIONS

1. How much was spent in total to support a indigent family to the nearest dollar? [For example, in Alaska $155.1 + $38.8 = $193.9 (thousand) was spent. Divide this by 17.4 = $11.184 (thousand) or $11,184 per indigent family]. Of the other states, which spent the most and the least provide income support for indigent families?

    MOST _____ , Amount per family $_____

    LEAST _____ , Amount per family $_____

2. What percent of the total cost was paid by indigent families (versus from taxpayer money)? [For example, in Wisconsin indigent families paid $425.1 (thousand) and the total was the taxpayer's $1,034.2 (thousand) plus that family's s $425.1 (thousand) or $1,459.3 (thousands). Divide the family's 's share by the total cost 425.1/1,459.3 = .291. Turn this into percentage rounded to a whole percent or 29%]. Of the other states listed, in which two did families pay the highest and in which two the smallest percent of the cost?

    2 HIGHEST _____, _____, % of total cost _____%, _____%

    2 LOWEST _____, _____, % of total cost _____%, _____%

3. What proportion of the total state population Indigent families? This is simply the total indigent familiesas a percent of state population. [For example, Oklahoma has 3,317 (thousands or about 3.3 million) and there were 213.3 (thousands) indigent families in Oklahoma, so 213.3/3317 = .064 or 6.4% of the total population are indigent famlies. Of the other states, in which two are indigent families the highest and in which two are students the smallest percent of the state's population?

    2 HIGHEST _____% , _____, %

    2 LOWEST _____% , _____, %

4. How much did the household pay for public indigent care? There is minor variation in household size by state, but let us assume the national average of 2.6 persons. [For example, Hawaii spent $242.7 (thousand) public spending, divide this by the state population 1,187 = .2045 (thousands). Turn this into dollars by multiplying it by 1000 or $204.50 per state resident. Next, multiply this by 2.6 to get the amount per household, = $531.70]. Of the other states, in which two did households pay the most and least to support public indigent care ?

    2 MOST _____, _____, Amount per indigent family $_____, $_____

    2 LEAST _____, _____, Amount per indigent family $_____, $_____

QUALITATIVE AND QUANTITATIVE SAMPLING

LEARNING OBJECTIVES

After studying Chapter 8 you will be able to do the following:
1. Distinguish between random assignment and random sampling;
2. Describe the meaning and use of a population, a population parameter, sampling elements, and sampling frames;
3. Describe various types of non-probability samples and explain when each is appropriate;
4. Explain why random sampling produces more representative samples than non-random sampling and the types of sampling qualitative research uses;
5. Understand the concepts of sampling distribution and confidence interval, and the basic principle represented by the Central Limit Theorem;
6. Calculate a sampling ratio and a sampling interval;
7. Describe when a systematic sample is appropriate and carry out a systematic sample;
8. Describe when a stratified sample is appropriate, carry out a stratified sample, and understand how stratifying a sample affects sample error;
9. Describe when a cluster sample is appropriate, carry out a cluster sample, and understand when PPS is necessary;
10. Understand the principles of choosing a sample size.

MATCHING DEFINITIONS

1. A type of random sample in which a researcher creates a sampling frame and uses a pure random process to select cases, each sampling element in the population will have an equal probability of being selected.
2. A diagram or "map" that shows the network of social relationships, influence patterns or communication paths among a group of people or units.
3. A characteristic of the entire population that is estimated from a sample.
4. A type of non-random sample in which the researcher begins with one case, then based on information about interrelationships from that case, identifies other cases, and repeats the process again and again.
5. A type of non-random sample in which the researcher first identifies general categories into which cases or people will be selected, then he or she selects cases reach a predetermined number of cases in each category.
6. A type of random sample in which the researcher first identifies a set of mutually-exclusive and exhaustive categories, then uses a random selection method to select cases for each category.
7. The name for a case or single unit to be selected.
8. The name for the large general group of many cases from which a researcher draws a sample and which is usually stated in theoretical terms.
9. The name for the large general group of many cases from which a sample is drawn and which is specified in very concrete terms.
10. A list of cases in a population, or the best approximation of it.
11. The number of cases in the sample divided by the number of cases in the population or the sampling frame, or the proportion of the population in the sample.
12. The inverse of the sampling ratio which is used in systematic sampling to select cases.
13. A method of randomly selecting cases for telephone interviews that uses all possible telephone numbers as a sampling frame.

14. A type of non-random sample in which the researcher uses a wide range of methods to locate all possible cases of a highly specific and difficult to reach population.
15. A type of non-random sample in which the researcher selects anyone he or she happens to come across.
16. A list of numbers which has no pattern in them and which is used to create a random process for selecting cases and other randomization purposes.
17. How much a sample deviates from being representative of the population.
18. A type of random sample that uses multiple stages and is often used to cover wide geographic areas in which aggregated units are randomly selected then samples are drawn from the sampled aggregated units, or clusters.
19. An adjustment made in cluster sampling when the each cluster does not have the same number of sampling elements.
20. A distribution created by drawing many random samples from the same population.
21. A law-like mathematical relationship which states: Whenever many random samples are draw from a population and plotted a normal distribution is formed, and the center of the such a distribution for a variable is equal to its population parameter.
22. A range of values, usually a little higher and lower than a specific value found in a sample, within which a researcher has a specified and high degree of confidence that the population parameter lies.
23. A type of random sample in which a researcher selects every kth (e.g., 12th) case in the sampling frame using a sampling interval.
24. A branch of applied mathematics or statistics based on a random sample. It lets a researcher make precise statements about the level of confidence she has in the results of a sample being equal to the population parameter.
25. A numerical estimate of a population parameter computed from a sample.
26. A smaller set of cases a researcher selects from a larger pool and generalizes to the population.
27. A type of non-random sample, especially used by qualitative researchers, in which a researcher selects unusual or non-conforming cases purposely as a way to provide greater insight into social processes or a setting.
28. People who engage in clandestine or concealed activities and who are difficult to locate and study.
29. A type of sample in which the sampling elements are selected using something other than a mathematically random process.
30. A type of sample in which the researcher uses a random number table or similar mathematical random process so that each sampling element in the population will have an equal probability of being selected.
31. A type of non-random sample in which a researcher tries to find as many relevant cases as possible, until time, financial resources, or his/her energy are exhausted, or until there is no new information or diversity from the cases.
32. A type of non-random sample in which the researcher selects specific times, locations or events to observe in order to develop a social theory or evaluate theoretical ideas.

MATCHING KEY TERMS FOR CHAPTER 8

_____ Central Limit Theorem
_____ Cluster Sampling
_____ Confidence Intervals
_____ Extreme Case Sampling
_____ Haphazard Sampling
_____ Hidden Populations
_____ Inferential Statistics
_____ Nonrandom Sample
_____ Parameter
_____ Population
_____ Probability Proportionate to Size [PPS]
_____ Purposive Sampling
_____ Quota Sampling
_____ Random Digit Dialing [RDD]
_____ Random Number Table
_____ Random Sample

_____ Sample
_____ Sampling Distribution
_____ Sampling Element
_____ Sampling Error
_____ Sampling Frame
_____ Sampling Interval
_____ Sampling Ratio
_____ Sequential Sampling
_____ Simple Random Sampling
_____ Snowball Sampling
_____ Sociogram
_____ Statistic
_____ Stratified Sampling
_____ Systematic Sampling
_____ Target Population
_____ Theoretical Sampling

Exercise 8.1

Draw a **two-stage random sample** of 60 names from the directory of student telephone numbers of your college or university. The directory is your <u>sampling frame</u>. If your directory separates students from others, just use student names, if it combines students with faculty and staff use the entire list of names.

Stage 1: Draw a <u>Simple Random Sample</u> of Clusters (Pages)

Count the number of pages with relevant names in the directory. Randomly select 10 pages by using the list of random numbers in Appendix B of the textbook OR use the *Sample* program on the CD that came with this workbook.

(1) **If you use Appendix B.** For Appendix B figure the number of digits for highest number of pages (e.g. 134 is three digits, 1034 is four digits, 86 is two digits). Now take one of the rows in Appendix B, and only look at the number of digits you need, starting at the end of the random number. For example, if the random number is 10819. If you only need two digits, ignore the "108" and take the "19." Go to the next number across or down and continue until you have ten numbers. If the number of pages you have is larger than a random number you select ignore it. For example, your telephone directory has 134 pages, three digits, but the three digit number from the first random number you get is 14568, or 568 for the three digits which is bigger than 134. Simply ignore that random number and go to the next one, until you come to a number that is 134 or smaller. Continue until you have 10 different numbers from 1 to the highest page number. These 10 constitute a simple random sample of pages.

(2) **If you use the *Sample* program.** For *Sample* put the CD in the microcomputer (NOTE: this is only available on IBM-compatible versions and requires an IBM-compatible microcomputer). For the population enter the number of relevant pages, for the <u>sample size</u> enter 10. The 10 number on the screen constitute a simple random sample of the pages. Photocopy the 10 pages to use in the next stage.

Stage 2: Draw a <u>Systematic Sample</u> from the Clusters

Each page is a <u>cluster</u> with <u>sampling elements</u>. In order to draw a <u>systematic sample</u> of six names from a cluster you must first compute the <u>sampling interval</u> for each page. Unless your telephone directory has exactly the same number of names on each page you have to compute a separate <u>sampling interval</u> for each of the 10 pages.

To compute a <u>sampling interval</u> count the total number of names on a page and divide it by your <u>sample size</u> for the cluster which is 6. For example, you find 110 names on a page 110/6 = 18.3. Round to the nearest whole number, or 18 in the example. Before you begin you need a random starting point. To get this you can use *Sample* or go back to Appendix B. For *Sample* just enter the total number of names on the page as your population and 1 as your sample size. For Appendix B you again need to know the total number of digits, but this time, pick a start number from the first digits of a random number. For example, if the random number is 98591 and you had 110 names on a page, you can't use the first three digits 985, so go across the list of random numbers until you come to a number that is 110 or smaller.

Beginning at your random start count down the interval. For example, with a random start of the 22nd name and <u>sampling interval</u> of 18, the 40th name is the first one in your sample. You would next go another 18 names to the 58th one and add it to your sample, and so forth.

Once you get to the end of the page you will not have 6 names for the sample unless your random number was smaller than your <u>sampling interval</u>. Just continue to the beginning, as if the first name on the page came after the last one. Repeat the process for each of the 10 pages.

Turn in the 10 photocopied pages. Show your work shown on them and the computations of sampling intervals for each and the 60 names you randomly selected.

Stage 3: Estimate the <u>Sampling Ratio</u>.

You now have a <u>sample</u> of 60 names. To estimate the <u>sampling ratio</u> you first need to compute the approximate number of names in the <u>sampling frame</u>. Take the average number of total names on the 10 pages and multiply this number by the total number of pages in the directory (you counted this for Stage 1). Now you have the <u>sample size</u> and an estimate of the population size. Compute the <u>sampling ratio</u>.

Exercise 8.2

Table 8.2 Illiteracy rates by sex, for ages 15-24 and 25+ for selected African nations

Country or area	Year	% 15-24 illiterate		% 25+ illiterate	
		women	men	women	men
Algeria	1987	37.8	13.8	79.5	50.2
Benin	1992	73.1	44.7	88.0	67.2
Botswana	1991	14.6 b	25.8 b	59.8 b	58.8 b
Burundi	1990	52.0	40.0	82.0	57.0
Cameroon	1987	29.0	15.0	68.0	43.0
Cape Verde	1990	13.6	10.1	62.5	34.9
Central African Rep.	1988	65.0	37.0	87.0	60.0
Congo	1984	17.2	7.6	69.9	41.4
Côte d'Ivoire	1988	62.2	40.1	85.3	63.4
Djibouti	1991	62.0	38.0	87.0	63.0
Egypt	1986	46.0 c	28.6 c	78.1 c	50.2 c
Equatorial Guinea	1983	23.9	9.3	64.5	28.7
Ethiopia	1984	68.5	50.7	89.2	73.6
Kenya	1989	13.9	8.1	54.2	26.0
Liberia	1984	66.3	37.2	89.2	64.3
Libyan Arab Jamahiriya	1984	19.7	2.1	83.2	37.3
Malawi	1987	50.9	29.5	74.6	37.2
Mali	1987	81.0	62.0	91.0	76.0
Mauritania	1988	61.8	43.1	82.6	59.4
Mauritius	1990	8.3	9.3	31.3	16.9
Morocco	1982	69.0	41.9	89.9	64.2
Mozambique	1980	74.7	36.0	93.8	65.8
Namibia	1991	9.6 d	14.3 d	35.0 d	26.8 d
Niger	1988	90.1	74.8	97.1	86.8
Reunion	1982	2.5	6.2	28.2	33.2
Senegal	1988	72.0	50.9	87.7	69.5
Seychelles	1987	2.0	3.0	21.0	23.0
South Africa	1980	15.0 e	14.7 e	30.1 e	26.4 e
Sudan	1993	40.5 f	22.1 f	74.1 f	42.6 f
Swaziland	1986	15.7	16.9	46.3	36.7
Togo	1981	64.1 g	26.8 g	90.4 a	67.9 a
Tunisia	1989	27.8	7.4	67.7	42.2
Uganda	1991	36.9	22.8	66.7	37.2
Zambia	1980	29.2 b	20.0 b	74.3 b	44.3 b
Zimbabwe	1992	3.5	5.6	32.8 h	16.7 h

Sources: [(Adapted from United Nations ©1997, Table 4-1]Prepared by the Statistics Division of the United Nations Secretariat from United Nations Educational, Scientific and Cultural Organization (UNESCO), *Statistical Yearbook* 1996 (Paris, 1996), *Compendium of Statistics on Illiteracy, 1995 edition* (Paris, 1995) and *Women's Indicators and Statistics Database (Wistat), Version 3, CD-ROM* (United Nations publication, Sales No. E.95.XVII.6). The United Nations Educational, Scientific and Cultural Organization (UNESCO) defines an illiterate person as someone who can not, with understanding, both read and write a short, simple statement on his or her everyday life.

Notes: a Ages 30+. b Illiterates are defined as persons with less than 5 years of schooling. c Data refer to Egyptian nationals only and exclude unemployed population. d Excluding unemployed population. e Not including Botphuthatswana, Transkei and Vida. f Data refer to Northern States only and do not include homeless and/or nomad populations. g Ages 15-29.h Ages 25-64.

INSTRUCTIONS

1. Take any 10 nations (haphazard sample) and compute average illiteracy rates for males and for women aged under 24.
2. Take every fifth nation (a systematic sample with a sampling interval of 5, beginning with Kenya). Compute the same illiteracy rates averages for 7 nations. Treat the list as a circle, so if you reach the end continue at the beginning.
3. Draw a simple random sample of 10 nations (see Exercise 8.1 on how). Compute the average illiteracy rates for the 10.
4. Compute the averages of the same two illiteracy rates for the population, or all 35 nations on the list.

Exercise 8.3

SNOWBALL SAMPLE: Locate 4 students who you have never seen with one another. Ask each in **Round 1** to name two other students at the same college with whom they are friends. For **Round 2** locate each of the friends and repeat (we can call these two friends A and B), only ask them not to name the first student who gave their name. For **Round 3** go to each of these students (A and B) and repeat, asking each to name two students who are friends. It has to be someone other than Round 2, but it could be any student named in Round 1. You will get 8 student names in round one, 16 in round two and 36 in round three, or 56 in total.

1. Draw a sociogram of your snowball sample
2. How many students in round three were present in Round 1?

ROUND 1	Student naming friends			
	Student 1	Student 2	Student 3	Student 4
Person named				
Close Friend 1	1.	2.	3.	4.
Close Friend 2	5.	6.	7.	8.

ROUND 2	Student naming friends			
	Student 1's Friend 1	Student 2's Friend 1	Student 3's Friend 1	Student 4's Friend 1
Person named				
Friend A	9.	10.	11.	12.
Friend B	13.	14.	15.	16.
	Student 1's Friend 2	Student 2's Friend 2	Student 3's Friend 2	Student 4's Friend 2
Person named				
Friend A	17.	18.	19.	20.
Friend B	21.	22.	23.	24.

ROUND 3	Student naming friends			
	1 F1, A	2 F1 A	3 F1, A	4 F1, A
Person named				
Friend X	25.	26.	27.	28.
Friend Y	29.	30.	31.	32.

	1 F1, B	2 F1 B	3 F1, B	4 F1, B
Person named				
Friend X	33.	34.	35.	36.
Friend Y	37.	38.	39.	40.

	1 F2, A	2 F2 A	3 F2, A	4 F2, A
Person named				
Friend X	41.	42.	43.	44.
Friend Y	45.	46.	47.	48.

	1 F2, B	2 F2 B	3 F2, B	4 F2, B
Person named				
Friend X	49.	50. **	51.	52.
Friend Y	53.	54.	55.	56.

Exercise 8.4

QUOTA SAMPLE:

Select two characteristics for quota groups (common ones are sex, age, race, year or class in college, general type of major). Cross classify the two characteristics to create four to six categories. For example,

Age Group	Male	female
Under 20		
20-22		
23 or higher		

Put a number in each category of the table for a total of 30 students. For example, 5 in each of the categories above would be 5 males under 20, 5 females under 20, 5 males 20-22 years old, etc.

Now go to a location with many students. Approach students one at a time and tell them that you are doing a quick survey and have to ask their age and major. Record the age, sex and major of each student you contact. Once you have "filled your quota" try to avoid asking people who look the same (e.g., if you need 5 females over 23 and have all 5, do not approach any more females who appear to be over 23). You may have to go to more than one location more than one time to "fill you quota." Stop asking once you have the number of people in each category you pre-set.

1. How many students in total did you have to contact in order to fill your quota?

2. Which category did you approach the most people, more than needed for your quota, in trying to get your quota filled?

3. Which category, if any, did you contact exactly the number needed to fill the quota and no more.

1. Ken Clark wanted to test the hypothesis: "White males who strongly oppose gun control laws and who own pistols are more likely to be racially prejudiced towards blacks than are white males who favor gun control laws and who do not own pistols." His **dependent variable** is:
   a. Gun ownership
   b. White males
   c. Racial prejudice towards blacks
   d. Gun control laws
   e. Insufficient information provided

2. Which of the following sets are **variables**?
   a. Male, Jewish, educational level
   b. Plumber, professor, dentist
   c. Occupation, political party preference, birthrate
   d. 21 years old, violent, social class
   e. None of the above

3. A researcher conducted a study of women's attitudes toward raising the tax on cigarettes. Her **unit of analysis** are:
   a. Individual women
   b. Attitudes
   c. Cigarettes
   d. Taxes
   e. None of the above

4. A researcher examined newspaper editorials from 20 major U.S. cities that dealt with rate of women who work after welfare reform. The **unit of analysis** was
   a. Welfare Reform
   b. Major cities
   c. Newspapers
   d. Newspaper editorials
   e. Women

5. If you went to a restaurant and saw the following lists of dessert choices which is **both mutually exclusive and exhaustive**?

<u>A</u>	<u>B</u>	<u>C</u>	<u>D</u>	<u>E</u>
Apples	Jello	Brownies	Rice Pudding	Apple Pie
Fruit	Bananas	Cookies	Ice Cream	Oatmeal
Cookies				
Cake	Ice Cream	Baked Sweets	Pie	Cherry Pie
Ice Cream	Grapes	Fruit	Fruit	Chocolate
Brownies				
Other	Pineapple	Other	Other	Cheese Cake

6. <u>Law of Comparative Judgement</u> is used in what type of scale or index?
   a. Semantic Differential
   b. Likert scale
   c. Bogardus social distance scale

d. Thurstone scale

e. Guttman Scale

Use the following model for question 7

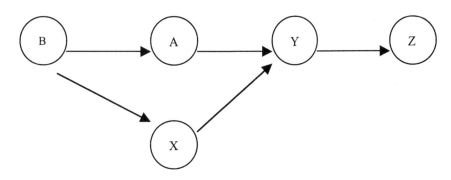

7. The dependent variable is symbolized by:

   a. X

   b. Y

   c. Z

   d. A

   e. B

use for 8 and 9

Hicks and Misra (1993, *American Journal of Sociology, 99*, 668-710) tested whether the "welfare effort in affluent postwar democracies" can be accounted for by the "use of government authority by the left" and "use of disruption by the working class." The authors tested the theory by looking at data on 18 large democracies for the years 1960-1982. They measured welfare effort as the "share of the gross national product" for welfare (e.g. education, social security, aid to the poor). They measured leftist power by the percent of cabinet positions held by left-wing political parties. For a measure of working class disruption, they used the number of "man-days" loss due to strikes and work stoppages. Their data for the share of the gross national product came from the International Labor Organization, data for leftist power and strikes came from previous studies by other researchers.

8. In this study, the **operational definition** of the **dependent variable** is:

   a. man-hours loss due to strikes and work stoppages

   b. welfare effort

   c. share of a nation's gross national product spent on welfare

   d. International Labor Organization

   e. use of government authority by the left

9. In this study, the **unit of analysis** is:

   a. the nation

   b. the strike or work stoppage

   c. the individual

   d. the welfare program

   e. the organization supplying data (e.g. International Labor Organization)

10. Dr. Ladysmith wants to develop a set of excellent questions to use in a study of gender role expectations. After working on it, she has come up with 118 possible questions, yet she only needs 20 of them for her questionnaire. What measurement technique should she consider given her situation?
   a. Bogardus Social Distance Scale
   b. Semantic Differential
   c. Thurstone Scale
   d. Likert Scale
   e. Guttman Scale

11. In measuring the percent of Japanese exchange students attending ten large universities in 2002, Noriko first got information from the Register's Office at each school. Next, she conducted a survey of 1,000 randomly selected students at each university and asked their nation of origin. Lastly, she asked the surveyed students to estimate the percentage of the students at their university who were from Japan. She found that all three measures gave very similar results for the three universities located in large cities, but at the other seven universities she got very inconsistent results. She felt she had problems with.
   a. Representative Reliability
   b. Equivalence Reliability
   c. Stability Reliability
   d. a and b
   e. a and c

12. You find the following number of domestic violence cases in four cities and their population size for 2002:

City	Cases	Population Size
City A	100	200,000 people
City B	150	300,000 people
City C	300	600,000 people
City D	500	1 million people

   Which city had the highest rate for domestic violence cases in 2002?
   a. City A
   b. City B
   c. City C
   d. City D
   e. All have the same rate

Use for 13 to 15

The Citizens Utility Board (CUB) is opposing a request for a rate hike by several utility companies. The utilities say rates have to be increased to guarantee their shareholders a 16 percent rate of return. CUB argues that utility companies are monopolies delivering a necessity, so the rate hike is too high, especially for low income families. CUB decides to get additional information for an upcoming Public Service Commission hearing and contracts with you to find out how much households spend on necessities. You are to check the amount spent last year on food (excluding meals eaten away from home), utilities (electricity and gas), and rent or house payments. CUB provided you with a list of all 1 million gas and electric residential customers from the utility companies. To draw the sample you took every 500th address on the list and recorded the total amount of last year's utility bill. Next, you asked the person calling him/herself the "head of the household" how much the household spent on groceries and rent or house payments.

13. In this study each address of a residential customer is your:
   a. Sampling frame

b. Population unit
c. Sampling interval
d. Sampling unit
e. Sampling element

14. How large is your sample?
    a. 200
    b. 500
    c. 2,000
    d. 2,500
    e. 5,000

15. What type of sampling was used?
    a. Cluster
    b. PPS
    c. RDD
    d. Stratified
    e. Systematic

16. Sally draws a sample to survey the residents at Friendlyville Nursing Home. The nursing home records show that there are 1,000 residents in the home. Sally's sample has 150 residents. What is her **SAMPLING RATIO**?
    a. .015
    b. 0.15
    c. 15
    d. 150
    e. Insufficient information given to calculate

17. We want to draw a sample of the employees at a large hospital and be certain that my sample contains people from all personnel categories: physicians, nurses, administrators, cleaning staff, technicians, etc. We want to use a kind of probability sample. Which type of sample is best, i.e. lowest sampling error?
    a. Simple random sampling   d. Stratified sampling
    b. Quota sampling   e. Accidental sampling
    c. Cluster sampling

18. Which of the following is NOT a condition that suggests you should be using Probability Proportionate to Size Sampling (PPS)?
    a. Cluster sampling is used
    b. Units (states, blocks, etc.) are of unequal size
    c. Snowball sampling is used
    d. a and c
    e. a and b

19. Which of the following is true?
    a. Reconstructed Logic and Logic in Practice are two terms for the same thing; there is no difference between them.
    b. Reconstructed Logic better describes what occurs in qualitative research.
    c. Logic in Practice better describes what occurs in quantitative research.
    d. Logic in Practice is research as it is actually carried out, it is informally communicated and less standardized.

e. c and d

20. Juanita, a qualitative researcher, interprets what she sees in a setting and brings some preliminary coherence to observations by putting them in a context of a stream of events. This is called,
   a. First order interpretation
   b. Second order interpretation
   c. Third order interpretation
   d. Technocratic perspective

CHAPTER 9

EXPERIMENTAL RESEARCH

LEARNING OBJECTIVES

After studying Chapter 9 you will be able to do the following:
1. Recognize the research questions and situations for which experimental research is most appropriate;
2. Describe random assignment, understand its purpose, and know how to randomly assign;
3. Discuss the parts of an experiment and the steps needed to conduct one;
4. Read design notation, recognize the design notation of major experimental designs, and translate a verbal description of an experiment into appropriate design notation symbols;
5. Describe factorial designs in a shorthand way and explain main and interaction effects;
6. Explain threats to internal validity;
7. Explain external validity and discuss the differences between experimental and mundane realism;
8. Discuss the problem of reactivity and how it relates to the use of double blind experiments;
9. Examine the results of an experimental design and make comparisons to recognize whether major threats to internal validity are present;
10. Explain why researchers use deception in experiments and the obligations that come with a researcher using it.

MATCHING DEFINITIONS
1. A false treatment or one that has no effect in an experiment. It is sometimes called a "sugar pill" that a subject mistakes for a true treatment.
2. The name for people who are studied and participate in experimental research.
3. A threat to internal validity when groups in an experiment are not equivalent at the beginning of the experiment.
4. What the independent variable in experimental research is called.
5. When a researcher gives a true explanation of the experiment to subjects after using deception.
6. A type of experimental design that considers the impact of several independent variables simultaneously.
7. Threats to internal validity due to subjects failing to participate through the entire experiment.
8. The group that receives the treatment in experimental research.
9. Dividing subjects into groups at the beginning of experimental research using a random process, so the experimenter can treat the groups as equivalent.
10. An experimental design in which the dependent variable is measured periodically across many time points, and the treatment occurs in the midst of such measures, often only once.
11. When an experimenter lies to subjects about the true nature of an experiment or creates a false impression through his/her actions or the setting.
12. A threat to internal validity that occurs when subjects in the control group modify their behavior to makeup for not getting the treatment.

3. What is the **DEPENDENT VARIABLE** in the study?

4. What are the **UNITS OF ANALYSIS** in the study?

Exercise 9.2

Dr. Johnson wanted to see whether tokens for bookstore purchases, listening to rock and roll or positive statements about personal appearance improved student self-esteem more than traditional counseling or no treatment at all over a six week period. She randomly assigned four groups of 30 students to two groups. In all four groups the control group received no special treatment.

In Experimental Group A she gave the students tokens that could be redeemed at the local bookstore for personal items such as pencils and paper, toothpaste and the like. In Experimental Group B she told the students about the history of rock and roll and gave them portable CD players with a large quantity of rock and roll music. She also encouraged them to listen to the music at least six hours per day. In Experimental Group C asked her assistants to make flattering statements about the physical appearance of students when the came into the lab. In Experimental Group D she placed the students in traditional counseling to improve self-esteem. NOTE: She measured Self-Esteem with a questionnaire in which self-esteem went from 0 = very negative to 100 = very positive.

		Self Esteem Score and (Number of Students)	
		Pretest	Posttest
A.	**Experimental**	**65 (15)**	**63 (13)**
	Control	60 (15)	66 (14)
B.	**Experimental**	**65 (15)**	**89 (14)**
	Control	45 (15)	79 (14)
C.	**Experimental**	**66 (15)**	**90 (6)**
	Control	65 (15)	67 (14)
D	**Experimental**	**64 (15)**	**88 (14)**
	Control	63 (15)	66 (15)

1. Which set suggests that *experimental mortality* is an issue? Why?
2. Which set suggests that *internal validity* is not a noticeable problem and the independent variable had an effect? Why?
3. Which set suggests that *selection bias* is a problem? Why?
4. What happened in the set leftover after you answered 1, 2 and 3?

Exercise 9.3

Locate two of the following four experimental research articles.

♦ Ford, T. & Tonander, G. (1998). The Role of Differential between groups and social identity in stereotype formation. *Social Psychology Quarterly, 61,* 372-384.

♦ Ong, A. & Ward, G. (1999). The Effects of Sex and Power Schemes, Attitudes Toward Women and Victim Resistance on Rape Attributions. *Journal of Applied Social Psychology, 29,* 362-376.

♦ Page, S. (1999). Accommodating Persons with AIDS: Acceptance and Rejection in Rental Situations. *Journal of Applied Social Psychology, 29,* 261-270.

♦ Rind, B. & Strohmetz, D. (1999). Effect on Restaurant Ripping of a Helpful Message Written on the Back of Customer's Checks. *Journal of Applied Social Psychology, 29,* 139-144.

Answer the following about the two articles:
1. Describe the subjects. How many groups were there? How were subjects assigned to groups?
2. What is the experimental design in design notation symbols?
3. What hypothesis (or hypotheses) was tested?
4. What was the treatment or independent variable? How was it introduced?
5. What was the dependent variable? How was it measured?
6. What possible problems with internal validity do you see in the experiment?

Exercise 9.4

Select a report of an experiment published in a scholarly journal since 1995. Good journals to check are, *Social Work Abstracts, Research on Social Work Practice, Social Services Research, Journal of Applied Social Psychology, or Journal of Experimental Social Psychology.* Attach a photocopy of the article.

1. Describe the subjects. How many groups were there? How were subjects assigned to groups?
2. What is the experimental design in design notation symbols?
3. What hypothesis (or hypotheses) was tested?
4. Was it a laboratory or field experiment?
5. What was the treatment or independent variable? How was it introduced?
6. What was the dependent variable? How was it measured?
7. Were there any "manipulation checks" used to evaluate the measures of variables?
8. What possible problems with internal validity do you see in the experiment?
9. What external validity problems do you see in the experiment?

Exercise 9.5

DESIGN AN EXPERIMENT: [Read all of the instructions first.]
1. Select a <u>topic</u> appropriate for an experiment in social work and narrow down the topic to a <u>research problem</u> or question appropriate for an experiment. Phrase it as a question.
2. Identify 1-2 specific <u>conceptual hypotheses</u> that are linked to the research question in #1.
3. Identify the <u>independent</u> and <u>dependent variables</u> (and any <u>intervening variables</u>) in each hypothesis in #2.
4. Provide a <u>conceptual definition</u> for each variable identified in #3.
5. Provide an <u>operational definition</u> for each variable identified in #3. Explain the operational definitions in specific detail. Provide detailed instructions so that another social worker could carry out the experiment without having to ask you any questions. For example, if the experimenter is going to talk to the subjects, provide a script. Include a step by step outline of everything in the experiment, including a <u>debriefing</u> if deception is used.
6. Identify 1-2 <u>empirical hypotheses</u> linked to the <u>conceptual hypotheses</u> in #2 using your <u>operational definitions</u>.
7. Provide a design for your experiment using <u>design notation</u> (X's and O's). Identify the type of <u>experimental design</u> you are using if you use a standard one.
8. Describe the setting (e.g., when and where, a student lounge or a classroom) and <u>units of analysis</u> used.
9. Discuss the <u>reliability</u> of the <u>operational dependent variable</u> and explain how you might check the reliability.
10. Discuss the <u>measurement validity</u> of the <u>operational dependent variable</u>.
11. Discuss at least three forms of <u>internal validity threats</u> that might occur in your experiment (e.g., history, maturation, etc.). Explain in detail how each might lead to false conclusions. Also discuss the experiment's <u>external validity</u>.

SURVEY RESEARCH

LEARNING OBJECTIVES

After studying Chapter 10 you will be able to do the following:
1. Understand the history, logic, and limitations of survey research methods;
2. Recognize errors in survey question writing and write survey questions that avoid the errors;
3. Understand the issues involved with asking threatening questions in survey research;
4. Know the purpose of a contingency question and how to use it appropriately;
5. Describe advantages and disadvantages of open versus closed-ended survey questions;
6. Explain the purpose and use of filter and quasi-filter survey questions;
7. Understand questionnaire design issues such as question order, layout, and questionnaire length;
8. Discuss principles of the Total Design Method;
9. Explain advantages and disadvantages of mail, telephone interview, and face-to-face interview surveys;
10. Understand the differences between a survey research interview and an ordinary conversation.

MATCHING DEFINITIONS

1. A problem in survey research question writing that occurs when a highly respected group or individual is linked to one of the answers.
2. The name of a survey research questionnaire when a telephone or face-to-face interview is used.
3. A problem in survey research that occurs when two ideas are combined into one question, and it is unclear whether a respondent's answer is for the combination of both ideas, or one or the other.
4. A follow-up question or action in survey research used by an interviewer to have a respondent clarify or elaborate on an incomplete or inappropriate answer.
5. A type of survey question in which the respondent goes to one or another later question based on his or her answer to the question.
6. A type of survey research question in which respondents must choose from a fixed set of answers.
7. A type of survey research question in which respondents are free to offer any answer they wish to the question.
8. A type of survey research question in which respondents are given a fixed set of answers to choose from, but in addition an "other" category is offered so that they can specify a different answer.
9. Survey research questions about non-existence people or events to check whether respondents are being truthful, or questions that appear more than once and are used to check a respondent's consistency.
10. A bias in survey research in which respondents are give a "normative" response or a socially acceptable answer rather than give a truthful answer.

11. A type of <u>survey research</u> question in which respondents are likely to cover up or lie about their true behavior or beliefs because they fear a loss of self-image or that they may appear to be undesirable or deviant.

12. A written document in <u>survey research</u> that has a set of questions given to respondents or used by an interviewer to ask questions and record the answers.

13. Respondents who lack a belief or opinion, but who give an answer anyway if asked in a <u>survey research</u> question, often their answers are inconsistent.

14. When <u>survey research</u> respondents compress time when answering about past events. They overreport recent events and underreport distant past ones.

15. An effect that occurs when a specific term or word used in a <u>survey research</u> question affects how respondents answer the question.

16. An effect in <u>survey research</u> that occurs when respondents tend to choose the last answer response offered.

17. An effect in <u>survey research</u> when respondents tend to agree with every question in a series rather than thinking through their answer to each question.

18. An effect in <u>survey research</u> in which respondents hear some specific questions before others, and the earlier questions affect their answers to later questions.

19. An effect <u>survey research</u> when an overall tone or set topics heard by a respondent affects how they interpret the meaning of subsequent questions.

20. A way to order <u>survey research</u> questions in a <u>questionnaire</u> from general ones to specific.

21. One or more pages at the beginning of a <u>questionnaire</u> with information about an interview or respondent.

22. A specialized technique in <u>survey research</u> that is used for very sensitive topics. With it a respondent randomly receives a question without the interviewer being aware of the question the respondent is answering.

23. A type of <u>survey research</u> question in which a set of questions are listed in a compact form together all questions sharing the same set of answer categories.

24. A type of <u>survey research</u> question that fails to include a choice such as "no opinion" or "don't know."

25. A type of <u>survey research</u> question that includes the answer choice "no opinion" or "don't know."

26. A type of <u>survey research</u> question in which respondents are first asked whether they have an opinion or know about a topic, then only the respondents with an opinion or knowledge are asked a specific question on the topic.

27. <u>Survey research</u> in which interviewer sits before a computer screen and keyboard, reads from the screen questions to be asked in a telephone interview, then enters answers directly into the computer.

28. An overall approach to writing <u>survey research</u> questions and interviewing in which a researcher makes participation as easy as possible and increases the response rate by giving respondents a feeling of importance.

29. A type of group interview in which an interviewer asks questions to the group, and answers are given in an open discussion among the group members.

MATCHING KEY TERMS FOR CHAPTER 10

___ Closed-Ended Question	___ Partially-Open Question
___ Computer Assisted Telephone Interviewing	___ Prestige Bias
(CATI)	___ Probe
___ Context Effects	___ Quasi-Filter Question
___ Contingency Question	___ Questionnaire
___ Cover Sheet	___ Random Response Technique
	(RRT)
___ Double-barreled Question	___ Recency effect
___ Floaters	___ Response Set
___ Focus Groups	___ Sleeper Question
___ Full-Filter Question	___ Social Desirability Bias
___ Funnel Sequence	___ Standard-Format Question
___ Interview Schedule	___ Telescoping
___ Matrix Question	___ Threatening Questions
___ Open-ended Question	___ Total Design Method (TDM)
___ Order Effects	___ Wording Effects

Exercise 10.1

Collect at least four mail survey questionnaires that have been sent to you, your parents, friends, and others during the past two months, or survey questionnaires that appeared in general circulation magazines or newspapers to be completed by the general public. Write a critique the questions in the questionnaire and its design based on the principles outlined in the textbook.

Exercise 10.2

1. Write a hypothesis with two variables that is appropriate for survey research about a non-sensitive issue appropriate for college students. Write two questions to measure each variable (four in total). Indicate whether each question is measuring an attitude, behavior, etc. Indicate whether the variable is measured at the nominal, ordinal, interval or ratio level.

2. Design and type a 15 item questionnaire for a face-to-face interview from beginning to end including the four questions from number 1. Include instructions to interviewers and respondents, order the questions appropriately, etc. Include at least one of each of the following. Also, identify the question for each by writing the type of question in parenthesis next to it.
    - a contingency question
    - a full filter question
    - a quasi-filter question
    - a partially open question
    - an open question
    - a closed question

3. Locate two college students who are strangers, after getting their permission, tape record an interview each person separately. After you are done, ask if they understood all questions

PRACTICE QUIZ 4, Chapters 9-10 (16 questions)

1. A scholarly article reports that researchers used computers when conducting telephone interviews. Interviewers sat at a computer and read questions off the screen and entered answers directly into the computers. What are the initials of the technique that was used?
   - a. RRT
   - b. RDD
   - c. TDM
   - d. DDT
   - e. CATI

2. You read about a researcher who had interviewers ask respondents to clarify answers. This is using a:
   - a. suppression poll
   - b. mutually exclusive
   - c. pseudosurvey
   - d. informed consent
   - e. probe

MATCHING CHOSE THE TYPE OF QUESTION FROM THE LIST a-h BELOW FOR DEFINITIONS 3 to 6.
   - a. socially desirable question
   - b. double-barreled question
   - c. leading question
   - d. threatening question
   - e. prestige bias in a question
   - f. sleeper question
   - g. contingency question
   - h. matrix question

3. Asking about two things in the same question, often creating confusion.
4. Asking about something that does not exist or about which a respondent could not know to determine whether respondents are overstating their knowledge.
5. Asking two or more questions, such that answering the first determines which question comes next.
6. Asking about behaviors or opinions that are well-respected and about which respondent often underreport.

7. In survey research when a respondent answers many questions by saying "agree" without carefully considering each and giving an honest answer it is called the:
   - a. recency effect
   - b. telescoping effect
   - c. response set effect
   - d. order effect
   - e. context effect

8. When comparing a positivist-masculine paradigm interview with a feminist-paradigm interview, the positivist interviewer is more likely to:
   - a. interview people in a group setting.
   - b. disclose to the respondent her own personal experiences or feelings.
   - c. avoid control and foster equality of status with the respondent.
   - d. use formally structured, closed-ended questions.
   - e. permit respondents to go in directions they wish and express themselves in ways with which they feel most comfortable.

9. Which of the following is part of the "naive assumption model" of survey research?
   - a. A respondent's true behavior often differs from what he/she says in an interview.
   - b. Respondents give more a more truthful answer if they first know the researcher's hypothesis.
   - c. Respondents often misunderstand questions from the way intended by the researcher.
   - d. Survey research often has wording, question order and related effects.

e. The interview situation and specific interviewer have no impact on respondent answers.

10. Which non-research interview often involves both the interviewer and interviewee joining in deceiving other observers and where the style of the interview is more important than any information revealed.
    a.   job interview   d. investigative interview
    b.   assistance interview   e. entertainment interview
    c.   journalistic interview

11. Jerry Jones the coach at Hometown High school is designing a training program for the track team. He knows that exercise A, B and C are recommended but is not sure which order he should have his team members train in (i.e. A, B, C, or C, A, B, etc). What type of experimental design would he use to test the relative effectiveness of the different training sequences?
    a. One-group pre-test, post-test   d. Classical experiment design
    b. Solomon 4-group design   e. Post-test only design
    c. Latin square design

12. The **double-blind** experiment is one in which:
    a. The experimenter's assistant who works with subjects does not know who is in the experimental or control group, but subjects in each group know which group they are in.
    b. The experimental subjects do not know that they are in the experimental group, but the control group subjects know which group they are in.
    c. Neither subjects in any group, nor the experimenter's assistant who works directly with subjects knows which is the experimental or control group.
    d. The control group subjects do not know that they are in the control group, but experimental group subjects know which group they are in.
    e. None of the above.

13. The diagram to the right represents the:
    a. Solomon Four-Group Design
    b. Classical experimental Design
    c. Static Group Comparison
    d. Interrupted Time Series Design
    e. Johnson's Test/Retest model

	O	X	O
	O		O
R			
		X	O
			O

USE FOR 14-16

Professor Suchi wanted to see replicate findings of high school students and test whether the degree of racial prejudice of white college students would be reduced if they worked on complex tasks in teams with highly capable racial minority students. She used a double-blind procedure with a classical experimental design. The control groups worked in all-white teams and prejudice was measured with an index of 10 attitude items measured using a 5-point Likert Scale. She had five sets of 8 person teams complete a series of complex tasks. Prejudice scores ranged from a low of 0 (non-prejudiced anti-racist attitudes) to 40 (extremely prejudiced and racist attitudes). Her results are below:

a. Experimental		20 [8]	19 [8]
Control		10 [8]	10 [8]
b. Experimental		20 [8]	10 [4]
Control		21 [8]	19 [8]
c. Experimental		20 [8]	8 [8]
Control		21 [8]	9 [9]
d. Experimental		21 [8]	10 [8]
Control		20 [8]	20 [8]

14. Which shows support for the hypothesis without internal validity concerns?
15. Which suggests experimental mortality problems?
16. Which suggests selection bias problems?

CHAPTER 11

NONREACTIVE RESEARCH AND SECONDARY ANALYSIS

LEARNING OBJECTIVES

After studying Chapter 11 you will be able to do the following:
1. Describe the basic logic of nonreactive measurement techniques;
2. Understand the purpose of content analysis and know when it is appropriate to use;
3. Understand coding systems and types of coding used with content analysis;
4. Explain the issue of intercoder reliability;
5. Describe topics appropriate for existing statistics research and potential problems or limitations of it;
6. Discuss validity and reliability issues in existing statistics research;
7. Explain why missing data are a concern in existing statistics research and ways to resolve it.
8. Appreciate the use of secondary data analysis.

MATCHING DEFINITIONS

1. Another name for <u>non-reactive measures.</u> It emphasizes that the people being studied are not aware of it because the measures do not intrude.
2. <u>Nonreactive</u> <u>measures</u> of the residue of the activity of people or what they leave behind.
3. <u>Nonreactive</u> <u>measures</u> of the wear or deterioration on surfaces due to the activity of people.
4. A set of instructions or rules used in <u>content analysis</u> to explain how to systematically convert the symbolic content from <u>text</u> into <u>quantitative data.</u>
5. The process of converting raw information or data into another form for analysis. In <u>content analysis</u> is means a system for determining how to covert symbolic meanings in <u>text</u> into another form, usually numbers
6. A general name for symbolic meaning within a communication medium measured in <u>content analysis</u>.
7. A type of <u>content analysis</u> coding in which a researcher first develops a list of specific words, phrases, or symbols then finds them in a communication medium.
8. A type of <u>content analysis</u> coding in which a researcher identifies subjective meaning such as general themes or motifs in a communication medium.
9. A U.S. government publication that appears annually and contains an extensive complication of statistical tables and information.
10. A survey of a <u>random sample</u> of about 1,500 U.S. adults that has been conducted in most years between 1972 and the present and is available for many researchers to analyze.
11. Measures in which people being studied are unaware that they are in a study.
12. Pages on which a researcher writes down what is coded in <u>content analysis</u>.
13. A method of watching what is happening in a social setting that is highly organized and follows systematic rules for observation and documentation.
14. When a person uses of too many digits in a quantitative measure in an attempt to create the impression that data is accurate or the researcher is highly capable.

MATCHING KEY TERMS FOR CHAPTER 11

___	Accretion Measures	___	Manifest Coding
___	Coding system	___	Nonreactive
___	Coding	___	Recording Sheet
___	Erosion Measures	___	*Statistical Abstract of the U.S.*
___	Fallacy of Misplaced Concreteness	___	Structured Observation
___	General Social Survey (GSS)	___	Text
___	Latent coding	___	Unobtrusive measures

Exercise 11.1

Use the CD that comes with the workbook for this exercise. Follow the instructions in the workbook preface and connect to the Internet, and that has either Netscape Navigator™ or Microsoft Explorer™. Once you see the table of contents, go to Chapter 11. Go to *Statistical Abstract of the United States* on the Internet [Note you may have to download a free copy of Acrobat if you do not already have one on your computer to read information sent to you]. Select four variables for which data is available on all 50 states [exclude the District of Columbia and U.S. possessions]. Take the four variables from at least three different sections/chapters (e.g., crime, education, recreation, etc.). Use the most recent data you can find.

Identify the eight states that are highest for each variable. Include the table number from which you obtained the data, the year of the data, and the source of the Table (e.g., Internet version of Statistical Abstract 2001). **Be careful** not to make errors in comparing data across states were *standardization* is necessary unless you first standardize the data. For example, if you locate the total amount spent in each state on education but fail to standardize by the state's population, the data is meaningless! Either locate data where this is not a problem or first standardize it yourself. If you standardize it, note Table sources for both the variable and the "base" for standardization.

Give a short (1-3 sentence) discussion of findings about which states on top ranked on the four variables. Type the rankings and your discussion of findings on a separate sheet of paper.

EXAMPLE WITH THREE VARIABLES

Data are from Internet version (1997)

Largest % increase in state population 1996-97 (Table 28)*	Percent of state population that with less than a H.S. education as of 1990 (Table 247)*	Percent of state population receiving Aid to Families with Dependent Children as of 1994 (Table 604)*
1. Nevada	1. Mississippi	1. New York
2. Arizona	2. Kentucky	2. California
3. Utah	3. West Virginia	3. Mississippi
4. Colorado	4. Arkansas	4. Michigan
5. Idaho	5. Alabama	5. Louisiana
6. Georgia	6. Tennessee	6. Kentucky

| 7. Texas | 7. Louisiana | 7. Tennessee |
| 8. Oregon | 8. South Carolina | 8. West Virginia |

* District of Columbia is excluded

Findings: None of the fastest growing states, in terms of population, are highly ranked among states with people who have low education or among states with high welfare (AFDC) rates Half the states that are highly ranked for low education levels are also top ranked for the high welfare rates. In general, it appears that people are not migrating in large numbers to states where many people are on welfare or have low education. States were a higher percentage of people have little education tend to be states were more of the population receive welfare.

Exercise 11.2

Locate the Historical Statistics of the U.S., Colonial Times to 1970. [You'll have to go to the library to get it]. In it find Table B143-144, the white and non-white infant mortality rate, 1915-1930. Beginning with 1930 and using only the even years plot two lines below, one for blacks and one for whites. For example, in 1930 white rate was 60.1 and the non-white rates was 99.9. You may want to use different colors or solid versus dashed lines, or you may want to make your own chart using graph paper. Complete the series up to 1996 by going to recent editions of the *Statistical Abstract of the United States*. [Paper or Internet versions].

Chart 1: Black and White Infant Morality Rates, 1930-1996

```
100 -
 95 -
 90 -
 85 -
 80 -
 75 -
 70 -
 65 -
 60 -
 55 -
 50 -
 45 -
 40 -
 35 -
 30 -
 25 -
 20 -
 15 -
 10 -
  5
  0 -
    1930 32 34 36 38 40 42 44 46 48 50 52 54 56 58 60 62 64 66 68 70 72 74 76 78 80 82 84 86 88 90 92 94 96
                Year
```

Now subtract the white and non-white rates and plot the size of the difference; for example, in 1930 99.9-60.1 = 39.8.

CHAPTER 12

ANALYZING QUANTITATIVE DATA

LEARNING OBJECTIVES

After studying Chapter 12 you will be able to do the following:
1. Describe the process of coding quantitative data and methods for cleaning the coded data;
2. Construct a frequency distribution, describe its purpose, and properly interpret or read different forms of the frequency distribution;
3. Calculate the three measures of central tendency and describe their characteristics;
4. Understand the concept of variation and interpret the standard deviation;
5. Understand the use of the z-score and calculate both the z-score of a score and the score corresponding to a z-score if given the mean and standard deviation;
6. Construct a scattergram and recognize various bivariate relationships in a scattergram;
7. Construct a bivariate percentaged table, describe the parts of a table, and properly interpret a simple bivariate percentaged cross-tabulation;
8. Interpret the meaning for a relationship of specific correlation coefficients;
9. Construct trivariate percentaged tables, understand the concept of statistical control and interpret trivariate tables in terms of the elaboration paradigm;
10. Understand the concept of statistical significance, the basic logic of Type I and Type II errors, and interpret the meaning of various levels of significance.

MATCHING DEFINITIONS

1. A document that describes the procedure for coding variables and their location in a format for computers.
2. A table that shows the cross-tabulation of two or more variables. Usually it shows bivariate quantitative data for variables in the form of percentages across rows or down columns for the categories of one variable.
3. A measure of central tendency for one variable that indicates the most frequent or common score.
4. A measure of central tendency for one variable indicating the point or score at which half the cases are higher and half are lower.
5. A measure of central tendency for one variable that indicates the arithmetic average, i.e., the sum of all scores divided by the total number of scores.
6. A measure of dispersion for one variable indicating the highest and lowest scores.
7. A measure of dispersion for one variable that indicates the percentage of cases at or below a score or point.
8. A measure of dispersion for one variable that indicates an average distance between the scores and the mean.
9. Paper with a printed grid into which a researcher records information so that it can be easily entered into a computer. It is an alternative to direct-entry method and using optical-scan sheets.
10. A display of numerical information on one variable that divides a circle into fractions by lines representing the proportion of cases in the variable's attributes.
11. Placing data for two variables in a contingency table to show the number or percentage of cases at the intersection of categories of the two variables.
12. The center part of a contingency table. It contains all the cells, but not the totals or labels.

13. A part of the <u>body of a table</u>. In a <u>contingency table</u> it shows the distribution of cases into categories of variables as a specific number or percentage.
14. A way to locate a score in a distribution of scores by determining the number of <u>standard deviations</u> it is above or below the <u>mean</u> or arithmetic average.
15. A name for the units that computers read which contain quantitative information on <u>variables</u> for one case or person.
16. A "third" <u>variable</u> that shows whether or not a <u>bivariate relationship</u> holds up to alternative explanations. It can occur before or between other <u>variables</u>.
17. A method of entering <u>data</u> into a computer by typing <u>data</u> without code or <u>optical scan sheets</u>.
18. A system for describing patterns evident among tables when <u>bivariate contingency table</u> is compared with <u>partials</u> after the <u>control variable</u> has been added.
18. A pattern in the <u>elaboration paradigm</u> in which the <u>partials</u> show the same relationship as in a <u>bivariate contingency table</u> of the <u>independent</u> and <u>dependent variable</u> alone.
20. A pattern in the <u>elaboration paradigm</u> in which the <u>bivariate contingency table</u> shows a relationship, but the <u>partials</u> show no relationship and the <u>control variable</u> is intervening in the <u>causal explanation</u>.
21. A pattern in the <u>elaboration paradigm</u> in which the <u>bivariate contingency table</u> shows a relationship, but the <u>partials</u> show no relationship and the <u>control variable</u> occurs prior to the <u>independent variable</u>.
22. A pattern in the <u>elaboration paradigm</u> in which no relationship appears in a <u>bivariate contingency table</u>, but the <u>partials</u> show a relationship between the <u>variables</u>.
23. A pattern in the <u>elaboration paradigm</u> in which the <u>bivariate contingency table</u> shows a relationship. One of the <u>partial tables</u> shows the relationship, but other tables do not.
24. Cleaning <u>data</u> using a computer in which the researcher looks at the combination of categories for two <u>variables</u> for logically impossible cases.
25. Cleaning <u>data</u> using a computer in which the researcher looks for responses or answer categories that cannot have cases.
26. A diagram to display the <u>statistical relationship</u> between two <u>variables</u> based on plotting each case's values for both of the <u>variables</u>.
27. The absence of a <u>statistical relationship</u> between two <u>variables</u>, i.e., when knowing the values on one <u>variable</u> provides no information about the values one will find on another <u>variable</u>. There is no <u>association</u> between them.
28. Statistical measures that deal with one <u>variable</u> only.
29. In <u>contingency tables</u> for three <u>variables</u>, tables that show the <u>association</u> between the <u>independent</u> and <u>dependent variables</u> for each category of a <u>control variable</u>.
30. A display of <u>quantitative data</u> for one variable in the form of rectangles where longer rectangles indicate more cases in a variable category. Usually it is used with discrete data and there is a small space between rectangles. They can have a horizontal or vertical orientation. They are also called bar graphs.
31. The effect of one <u>variable</u> (usually <u>independent</u>) on another (usually <u>dependent</u>) after the impact of one or more <u>control variables</u> that affects both has been taken into consideration and statistically removed.
32. The totals in a <u>contingency table</u>, outside the <u>body of a table</u>.
33. A sheet with organized spaces or dots that one can fill in usually with a pencil. A special machine can read information from it into a computer.
34. A set of numbers researchers use as a simple way to measure the degree to which a <u>statistical relationship</u> results from random factors rather the existence of a true relationship among <u>variables</u>.

35. A distribution of cases among the categories of a <u>variable</u> which is not <u>normal</u>, i.e., not a "bell shape." Instead of an equal number of cases on both ends, more are at one of the extremes.
36. A table that shows the distribution of cases into the categories of one <u>variable</u>, i.e., the number or percent of cases in each category.
37. A graph of connected points showing the distribution of how many cases fall into each category of a <u>variable</u>.
38. Statistical measures that involve two <u>variables</u> only.
39. Expressing whether or not two or more <u>variables</u> affect one another based on the use of elementary applied mathematics, i.e., whether there is an <u>association </u>between them or <u>independence.</u>
40. The idea that two <u>variables</u> vary together, such that knowing the values on one <u>variable</u> provides information about values found on another <u>variable</u>.
41. An <u>association</u> between two <u>variables</u> that is positive or negative across the attributes or levels of the <u>variables</u>. When plotted in a <u>scattergram </u>the basic pattern of the <u>association</u> forms a straight line, not a curve or other pattern.
42. A relationship between two <u>variables</u> such that as the values of one <u>variable</u> increase, the values of the second show a changing pattern, e.g., first decrease then increase then decrease. It is not a <u>linear relationship</u>.
43. A general type of simple statistics used by researchers to describe basic patterns in the <u>data</u>.
44. A set of rules created by a quantitative researcher for assigning numbers to specific variable <u>attributes</u>, usually in preparation for statistical analysis and carefully recorded in a <u>code book</u>.
45. A "bell-shaped" <u>frequency polygon</u> for a distribution of cases, with a peak in the center and identical curving slopes on either side of the center. It is the distribution of many natural-occurring phenomena and is a basis of much statistical theory.
46. One or more columns in <u>data</u> already organized for a computer representing the location of information on a specific <u>variable</u>.
47. The logical error of falsely accepting the <u>null hypothesis</u>.
48. The logical error of falsely rejecting the <u>null hypothesis</u>.
49. A way to discuss the likelihood that a finding or <u>statistical relationship</u> in a <u>sample</u> results is due to the random factors rather than due to the existence of an actual relationship in the entire <u>population</u>.

MATCHING KEY TERMS FOR CHAPTER 12

___ Bar Chart	___ Marginals
___ Bivariate statistics	___ Mean
___ Body of a table	___ Median
___ Cell of a table	___ Mode
___ Code sheets	___ Net effect
___ Codebook	___ Normal Distribution
___ Coding Procedure	___ Optical scan sheet
___ Contingency cleaning	___ Partials
___ Contingency table	___ Percentile
___ Control variable	___ Pie Chart
___ Covariation	___ Possible code cleaning
___ Cross-tabulation	___ Range
___ Curvilinear relationship	___ Replication pattern
___ Data Field	___ Scattergram
___ Data Records	___ Skewed distribution
___ Descriptive statistics	___ Specification pattern
___ Direct entry method	___ Standard Deviation
___ Elaboration paradigm	___ Statistical relationship
___ Explanation pattern	___ Statistical significance
___ Frequency distribution	___ Suppressor Variable Pattern
___ Frequency polygon	___ Type I error
___ Independence	___ Type II error
___ Interpretation pattern	___ Univariate statistics
___ Level of Statistical Significance	___ Z score
___ Linear relationship	

Exercise 12.1

Use the CD that comes with the workbook for this exercise. Follow the instructions in the workbook preface and connect to the Internet using either Netscape Navigator™ or Microsoft Explorer™. Once you see the table of contents, go to the Chapter 12. Click on the **Statistics Textbook on-line**. You will see a list of topics in the sidebar to the left. Your textbook only covers the first two of these topics. Click on **Elementary Concepts**. Scroll down to the list of highlighted topics in this section. You might want to review concepts, such as independent versus dependent variables. Go to the section called Baby Boys to Baby Girls Ratio. Read the material around it and write a short explanation of what the author is talking about here. You might want to scan some other topics for fun. There are some "moving" images, such as in the discussion of the Normal Distribution.

Exercise 12.2

Use the CD that comes with the workbook for this exercise. Follow the instructions in the workbook preface and connect to either Netscape Navigator™ or Microsoft Explorer™. Once you see the table of contents, go to Chapter 12. Go to **fun, interactive web site**. Answer the questions and enter the exhibit. Answer the following three questions:

- "What's blood got to do with it?"
- What can go wrong?
- Who won the election?

Exercise 12.3

Use the CD that comes with the workbook for this exercise. Follow the instructions in the workbook preface and connect to the Internet using either Netscape Navigator™ or Microsoft Explorer™. Once you see the table of contents, go to Chapter 10, scroll to the bottom where there is a red arrow, click on the red arrow to go to the second survey research page. Go to GSS for the **General Social Survey.** Go to Data Applications-Extract Analyze. Select either the University of Michigan or the University of California-Berkeley. Go to Generate Descriptive Statistics, Frequencies and Cross Tabulations.

- In Statistic Select   FREQ
- In Weight Select   NO
- Enter Variable Name (Space delimited just means put a space between variable names): CLASS, RACE, DEGREE

Look at the results and print them out. Write a short description of what you see in the table. Now return to the statistics selection section.

- In Statistic Select   CROSS-TAB 1x1
- In Weight Select   NO
- Enter Variable Names: Select one Independent Variable name from the list below and two dependent variables.

Look at the results and print them out. Write a short description of what you see in the table.

INDEPENDENT VARIABLES
CLASS - Social Class, SEX - Male or Female, DEGREE - Highest educational degree, RACE - Racial identity

DEPENDENT VARIABLES
Abortion Attitudes

    ABPOOR - Is Abortion acceptable if the woman is poor and cannot afford to raise child?

    ABDEFECT - Is Abortion acceptable if the fetus has serious defect?

    ABRAPE - Is Abortion acceptable if pregnancy was the result of the woman being raped?

    ABSINGLE - Is Abortion acceptable if the woman is unmarried?

Religious Practice

    ATTEND - Frequency of attending religious services.

    PRAY - Frequency of praying.

Satisfaction

    SATFAM - Satisfaction with family

    SATCITY- Satisfaction with city/community

    SATJOB - Satisfaction with job

Sexual Relations

    PREMARSX - Premarital sex

TEENSEX - Sex among teenagers
XMARSEX - Extra-marital sexual relations
Politics
RACPRES - Vote for Black Presidential candidate
FEPRES - Vote for Women President candidate
Crime and Law
CAPPUN - Support/oppose capital punishment
GUNLAW - Support/oppose gun control laws

Exercise 12.4

Use the CD that comes with the workbook for this exercise. Follow the instructions in the workbook preface and connect to the Internet using either Netscape Navigator™ or Microsoft Explorer™. Once you see the table of contents, go to Chapter 10, scroll to the bottom where there is a red arrow, click on the red arrow to go to the second survey research page.
Go to the **National Election Survey.** Click on the Web Site Index [near the top] and go to the NES Guide to Public Opinion and Electoral Behavior, and to Index of first-level tables. This creates bivariate tables from the NES. dataset.
- Select three questions from one of the following: Race Issues, Social Welfare or Social Issues. These are your **Dependent Variables.**
- Click on Social Category to see tables of the question by demographic and political factors. Print out and discuss the following four categories (these are your **Independent Variables**) gender, race, education level and liberal/conservative identification

d. Compare answers to two different variables for logically Impossible combinations (e.g. males listed as given birth to children)

e. Marking a sheet with a black pencil so that the sheet can be "read" by a special machine and the information put into a computer

7. What is the MEDIAN of the following values: 8, 12, 9, 15, 17, 11, 13, 14, 7.

a. 12

b. 17

c. 4.5

d. 5

e. There is no median in this data

8. Raw Frequency of population per MD and Infant Mortality, 2000 in the 25 richest nations

Number of People per Medical Doctor	Infant Mortality Rate (Deaths per 1,000 Births)			
	5-6	7	8	9-10
700 +	1	2	1	0
600-699	1	2	0	0
500-599	0	0	1	1
400-499	1	2	2	1
200-399	0	2	4	4
TOTAL	3	8	8	6

Looking at the table above, which is the most accurate interpretation of what it shows?

a. The fewer people each MD has to serve, the lower the infant mortality rate, but the relationship is moderate.

b. There is no relationship between number of MD's and infant mortality.

c. The more people each MD has to serve, the higher the infant mortality rate, but the relationship is moderate.

d. The more people each MD has to serve, the lower the infant mortality rate, but the relationship is moderate.

9. Raw Frequency of population per MD and Infant Mortality in the 25 poorest nations

Infant Death Rate per 1,000 births	Population per Medical Doctor			
	under 3,000	3,000 to 10,000	10,000 to 19,000	20,000 and more
120 or more	0	0	1	6
100-119	0	0	2	2
80-99	1	4	1	0
under 80	4	4	0	0
Total	5	8	4	9

Looking at the table above, which is the most accurate interpretation of what it shows?

a. The fewer people each MD has to serve, the lower the infant mortality rate.

b. There is no relationship between number of MD's and infant mortality.

c. The more people each MD has to serve, the higher the infant mortality rate.

d. The more people each MD has to serve, the lower the infant mortality rate.

e. a and c

10. Data on smoking cigarettes and level of education show a negative relationship. When age is added as a control variable, with four age categories (16-26, 27-44, 45-58. 59 and

older), the relationship disappears in two partials (48-58 and 59 and older), but remains in two others. Using the elaboration paradigm, what do we say is going on?
a. Replication
b. Interpretation
c. Elaboration
d. Specification
e. Suppressor Variable

11. Hans Tschetter examined the FBI Crime Reports for a 30 year period and claimed that the number of sexual assaults increased. After examining the same reports more carefully, Cheryl Jones claimed that the reporting the crimes, not the incidence of sexual assault itself, increased because the FBI reports only measure crimes reported to police. This illustrates:
a. The problem of reliability in using existing statistics
b. The problem of validity in using existing statistics
c. The need to replicate existing statistics
d. The ecological fallacy
e. All of the above

12. Jose Garcia has a list of different measures on the Hispanic influence in the Atlanta area. He asked you to identify the one that is NOT an unobtrusive measure, which one is it?
a. The wear on novels in the Atlanta Public Library written in Spanish
b. Walking down a street in Atlanta and noticing that most of the signs in stores in a neighborhood are in Spanish
c. A list of votes supporting bills on bilingual education in the Georgia state legislature with the area represented by the legislator noted.
d. A box of 300 letters that were written by Chicanos living in Atlanta to relatives living in Mexico between 1980 and 1985.
e. A 4-page questionnaire written in Spanish distributed to residents of a neighborhood.

Below are data from a SPSS printout for a Crosstabulation between a dependent variable, **Grade** in a research methods course (Average or High) and an independent variable, whether students had been given a **prescription for Valium** or a **Placebo**. We have decided the independent variable (MEDS) can best be thought of as nominal level, we have not used probability (random) sampling, nor have we met any of the other assumptions required to use parametric statistics. So we have selected a nonparametric statistic, Chi Square, and we are using .05 as our cutoff point.

GRADE * MEDS Crosstabulation

Count

		MEDS		
		Placebo	Valium	Total
GRADE	Average	12	2	14
	High	17	19	36
Total		29	21	50

Chi-Square Tests

	Value	df	Asymp. Sig. (2-sided)	Exact Sig. (2-sided)	Exact Sig. (1-sided)
Pearson Chi-Square	6.131[b]	1	.013		
Continuity Correction[a]	4.653	1	.031		
Likelihood Ratio	6.751	1	.009		
Fisher's Exact Test				.024	.013
Linear-by-Linear Association	6.008	1	.014		
N of Valid Cases	50				

a. Computed only for a 2x2 table

b. 0 cells (.0%) have expected count less than 5. The minimum expected count is 5.88.

13. We have a hypothesis H1: Students who received a Valium prescription will have higher final grades than those who received a placebo. Ho: There is no relationship between type of meds and final grade. What should we conclude about our findings if our Type I error level for this test is set at .05?

a) We have a very strong negative relationship which is significant at the .99 level
b) We have failed to reject the null hypothesis at the .05 level
c) We have evidence in this study at the .05 level for supporting Ho.
d) Chi Square indicates a significant relationship at the .05 level

CHAPTER 13

FIELD RESEARCH

LEARNING OBJECTIVES

After studying Chapter 13 you will be able to do the following:
1. Explain when field research is an appropriate research technique;
2. Describe the steps in conducting a field research study;
3. Discuss the issues of site selection and access in field research;
4. Explain how field researchers maintain social relations in the field setting and several approaches they adopt to gather information;
5. Discuss the various social roles and degrees of involvement a field researcher can adopt;
6. Describe techniques for resolving conflicts in the field and writing field notes;
7. Discuss reliability and validity in field research;
8. Describe differences between field research and survey research interviews;
9. Explain the kind of questions asked in field research interviewing and use of informants;
10. Discuss at least two ethical issues specific to field research.

MATCHING DEFINITIONS

1. In field research, false or made-up names researchers put in field notes to protect the identity of the people they study.
2. The special language or terminology of a subculture or group that interacts regularly.
3. What happens when a researcher in field research gets overly involved and loses all distance or objectivity and becomes like the people being studied.
4. A person in an official or unofficial role who controls access to a setting.
5. The principle that researchers should examine events as they occur in natural, everyday on-going social settings.
6. When one or more people in a field site engage in actions and say things that give an impression or appearance that differs from what is actually occurring.
7. A technique in field research in which researchers maintain relations in a field site by pretending to be interested and excited by the activities of those studied even though they are actually uninterested or very bored.
8. Techniques in field research used by researchers to make the people being studied feel more comfortable with the research process and to help them accept the researcher's presence.
9. A technique in field research in which researchers study a field site by mentally adjusting to "see" it for the first time or as an outsider.
10. Notes taken in field research that attempt to include all details and specifics of what the researcher heard or saw in a field site. They are written in a way that permits multiple interpretations later.
11. When social rules and patterns of behavior in a field site do not operate as expected, or are purposely disrupted or broken by a researcher. The disruptions often reveal a great deal about social meanings and relationships.
12. A technique early in field research when a researcher removes his or her past assumptions and preconceptions to become more open to events in a field site.
13. When one or more people being studied in field research refuse to cooperate with the researcher or to become involved in the study.

14. In <u>field research</u>, what a researcher inconspicuously writes while in the <u>field site</u> on whatever is convenient in order to "jog the memory" later.

15. In <u>field research</u>, the researcher writes direct observation notes in a way that keeps what he or she actually observed separate from what he or she infers or believes occurred.

16. When a researcher conducting <u>field research</u> pretends to be less skilled or knowledgeable in order to learn more about a <u>field site</u>.

17. The written notes a qualitative researcher takes during <u>data</u> collection and afterwards to develop concepts, themes, or preliminary generalizations.

18. The one or more natural locations where a researcher conducts <u>field research</u>.

19. A way to achieve <u>reliability</u> of <u>data</u> in <u>field research</u> in which the researcher cross-checks and verifies <u>qualitative data</u> using multiple sources of information.

20. Open-ended interviews, usually recorded, with one person who describes their entire life. It often has therapeutic benefits for the person interviewed and creates <u>qualitative data</u> on the life cycle. It can be considered a subtype of <u>oral history</u>.

21. A type of question asked in early in <u>field research.</u> The researcher seeks basic information (e.g., who, what, when, where) about the <u>field site</u>.

22. A type of question in <u>field research</u> interviews in which the researcher attempts to verify the correctness of placing terms or events into the categories of the meaning system used by people being studied.

23. A type of interview question asked late in <u>field research</u> in which the researcher verifies the correctness of distinctions found among categories in the meaning system of people being studied.

24. Demonstrating the authenticity and trustworthiness of a <u>field research</u> study by the researcher "passing" as a member of the group under study.

25. A way to demonstrate the authenticity and trustworthiness of a <u>field research</u> study by having the people who were studied, i.e., members, read and confirm as being true that which the researcher has reported.

26. A way a researcher can demonstrate the authenticity and trustworthiness of a <u>field research</u> study by fully disclosing his or her actions and procedures in depth as they occurred over time.

27. The idea that a field researcher may only be able to see and learn about public, non-controversial events at first, but with time and effort may gain entry to more hidden, intimate and controversial information and thoughts.

28. An approach to social science that combines philosophy, <u>social theory</u>, and method to study common sense knowledge. Researchers using it study ordinary social interaction in small-scale settings to reveal the rules that people use to construct and maintain their everyday social reality.

29. An approach to <u>field research</u> that emphasizes providing a very detailed description of a different culture from the viewpoint of an insider in that culture in order to permit a greater understanding of it.

30. A page at the beginning of interview or field notes with information on the date, place of observations, interviews, the context, etc.

31. In <u>field research</u>, a researcher who learns much about weaker members of society whose views are rarely heard often gets accused of "bias" when presenting findings. At the same time opposing views presented by powerful people are accepted as "unbiased" simply because of their high social status.

32. When a researcher in <u>field research</u> learns of illegal, unethical or immoral actions by the people in the <u>field site</u> that is not widely known.

33. In <u>qualitative data</u> collection, the researcher's attempt to capture all the details of a social setting in a highly detailed descriptions to capture and convey an intimate feel for the setting and the inner lives of people in it.

33. A passing reference made by a person in a <u>field site</u> that actually indicates a very important event or feeling.

35. A way to demonstrate the authenticity and trustworthiness of a <u>field research</u> study by showing that the researcher's descriptions of the field site matches those of the members from the site and that the researcher was not a major disturbance.

NAME _____ DATE

MATCHING KEY TERMS FOR CHAPTER 13

___ Acceptable incompetent
___ Access ladder
___ Analytic Memos
___ Appearance of interest
___ Argot
___ Attitude of Strangeness
___ Breakdown
___ Competent insider performance
___ Contrast question
___ Defocusing
___ Descriptive question
___ Direct Observation Notes
___ Ecological validity
___ Ethnography
___ Ethnomethodology
___ External Consistency
___ Face sheet
___ Field site

___ Freeze outs
___ Fronts
___ Gatekeepers
___ Go native
___ Guilty knowledge
___ Hierarchy of credibility
___ Jotted Notes
___ Life History interview
___ Marker
___ Member validation
___ Natural history
___ Naturalism
___ Normalize social research
___ Pseudonyms
___ Separation of inference
___ Structural question
___ Thick description

Exercise 13.1

Do this exercise in teams or individually. It gives you minimal "first hand" experience in field research. Conduct 4 hours of field observation and take detailed field notes. If your instructor has you work in teams, all team members should observe the same setting at different times. Observe on 3 different days with each observation period at least one hour long. A key to success is to think about the site you select, put effort and involvement into observation, take detailed and in-depth notes, and seriously reflect about the experience. Separate your field notes as described in the textbook and make sparing use of "jotted notes."

Part 1: Locate a pubic setting and gain access. Write a 1-2 paragraph explanation of why the site was chosen, whether the first site was selected, and if not why. Also discuss any access problems encountered. Characteristics of a <u>good site</u> for observation include: (1) it has 1-2 small to moderate sized spaces or rooms; (2) it has 5 to 25 people; (3) there are few college students there; (4) it is a new and unknown place, you "should" feel a little uncomfortable; (5) people at the site talk to each other and have interacted with each other in the past. **Better settings** are: small churches, court rooms, health clubs, bingo parlors, bowling alleys, small local bars or restaurants, small town banks, and work settings. **Worse settings** are: large supermarkets, shopping malls, the large waiting areas, almost any place on a college campus. Describe the setting in detail in the large waiting areas, almost any place on a college campus. Describe the setting in detail in 1-2 pages. Be explicit and describe the color, size, appearance, odors, sounds, etc. For example, instead of, "there was a cross in the front of the church" say "at the front of the church, backed by a stained class window through which the morning sun shone, there was a gold colored cross about 20' tall and about 10' wide which hung just above the alter with wires attached to the ceiling."

Part 2: Conduct field observation and apply techniques described in the textbook. Observe very closely, adopt an attitude of strangeness, and take only very few "jotted notes" in the field, write up extensive field notes shortly after leaving the field. Separate the field notes into three sections: (1) direct observation, (2) interpretation, (3) analytic notes/personal journal. Always include the date, time, and name of the observer at the top of each page of field notes and attach the "jotted notes" to the field notes they correspond to. Conduct a short (10 minute) "unstructured interview" with an "informant."

HINTS FOR WRITING GOOD FIELD NOTES

- Be specific. Do not say, "Most people wore blue jeans." Instead say, " I saw five people in blue jeans, and two people whose pants I could not see."
- Be clear. Do not say, "It was intense" or "nice." Describe what you actually saw/heard in precise terms. Also do not say "This store's attitude towards . . ." Stores do not have attitudes, people do.
- Do not make unfounded assumptions. For example, do not say, "a group of 10 college students arrived together" say "a group of 10 people who were 18-22 years old arrived together at about 10:15." Only call individuals college students if you have specific information suggesting that, and then specify what it is (she is in my history class).
- Be explicit. Assume you are writing for a reader who knows nothing about the social or physical setting.

Part 3: Write a 1-2 page summary-evaluation of the observation. It should include: how you would do things differently if you were to begin over again, types of things you think you missed in the field notes, themes or ideas you would focus on if you were to continue the observation for an additional 20 hours, your personal feelings, insights, reactions or thoughts while doing the observation, your overall evaluation of what you learned, or failed to learn, from this experience and how you might use the learning elsewhere.

Exercise 13.2

Go to your college library and locate a scholarly article in which field research was used. Two especially good journals to look are The Journal of Contemporary Ethnography and Qualitative Sociology, although you may find them in other journals (look at the references for Chapter 13).

Attach a photocopy of the first page of the article and give a full citation of it:

Describe the main topic of the study:

What is the field setting or site where most observation took place?

How long did the observation take place?

What types of people or social interaction did the researcher focus on?

How did the field researcher gain access to the field setting?

What social role did the researcher assume in the field setting?

Identify two major themes or generalizations from the study.

CHAPTER 14

EVALUATION RESEARCH

LEARNING OBJECTIVES

After studying Chapter 14 you will be able to do the following:

1. Identify the types of questions for which evaluation research is most suited;
2. Describe when an agency or practice setting is ready for an evaluation and whether to use internal or external evaluators;
3. Recognize the difference between formative and summative evaluation;
4. Sketch a basic logic model for an evaluation of agency or program already known to you;
5. Describe how impact/outcome evaluations differ from performance, process and cost benefit analysis;
6. Sketch a diagram for a clinical problem that could be evaluated using the AB, ABA, and ABAC single case designs;
7. Describe how empowerment evaluation differs from more traditional approaches;
8. Identify the different types of needs that can be evaluated using needs assessments;
9. Describe the role of diversity in an agency known to you and tell whether the Euro-Male paradigm has been dominant in that setting.

MATCHING DEFINITIONS
1. An evaluation that examines how much a program and/or it's components cost.
2. A graphical representation of an agency program or set of interventions that schematically shows relationships between program efforts, interventive activities and outcomes.
3. The extent to which objectives are realized.
4. All of those individuals whose interests may be effected by or who may be interested in a program or agency outcome
5. The logic of explanation that involves a topic, contrast class and relevance relation.
6. Gathering information to determine whether individuals or families in a particular neighborhood or community have been receiving the services they require.
7. The application by a social worker of selected components of experimental evaluation design to a single case or individual in a clinical setting.
8. The difference between a program prior to an intervention and the expected or desired level of effectiveness after the intervention.
9. Resources such as supplies, production support and labor.
10. All of those clients and potential clients who are the focus of a needs assessment or community study.
11. An evaluation focus that examines existing agency or program information to determine, retrospectively, what a given set of interventions or program(s) accomplished.
12. A single subject design that utilizes a control period and an experimental period, while the clinician measures and compares the client's condition before and during the intervention, then repeats this process a second time.
13. Assessing the characteristics of those who have been receiving services in relation to those who might benefit if they also were to receive services.
14. An evaluation that involves clients as 'co-researchers' so that more influence will come to reside with them.

15. The relationship between achievement of objectives and expenditure of time, energy and resources.
16. The name for the major category or group selected "in comparison" in evaluation research.
17. An evaluation that looks at existing records to determine how well a program has functioned or performed.
18. An evaluation that examines a limited number of clients or cases usually involving the collection of information from in-depth interviews with clients.
19. Asking clients their opinions and beliefs about services they feel they will benefit from.
20. An evaluation strategy that involves gathering a small set of social workers, clients, or community members together to discuss a question or concern in a face-to-face group setting.
21. The experiences of a social work researcher looking inward.
22. An evaluation focus that will examine how interventions, programs or services can be made more effective in the future (prospectively).
23. A single subject design with one period that is analogous to a control group and one period analogous to an experimental period; while the clinician measures and compares the client's condition before and during the intervention.
24. An evaluation method that seeks to understand a program or agency from the point of view of local cultures and subcultures.
25. An evaluation that would divide inputs by outputs.
26. Doing exactly the opposite of what would be expected in order to gain better insight into what is going on.

NAME _____ DATE

MATCHING KEY TERMS FOR CHAPTER 14

___ A-B design
___ A-B-A-B- design
___ Case study
___ Comparative need
___ Contrast class
___ Cost study
___ Effectiveness
___ Efficiency
___ Empowerment
___ Erotetics
___ Ethnography
___ Felt Need
___ Focus Group
___ Formative Evaluation
___ Gap effectiveness

___ Input
___ Intuition
___ Logic Model
___ Needs assessment
___ Performance evaluation
___ Productivity assessment
___ Single-case design
___ Stakeholders
___ Summative Evaluation
___ Target Population
___ Tricksterism

Exercise 14.1

Read over the discussion on logic models and study the examples given. Sketch a basic logic model for an evaluation of an agency or program already known to you. If you have not yet had experience in an agency setting, draw up a hypothetical logic model for a program you might someday be involved in.

Exercise 14.2

After reviewing the material in Chapter 14 on single case designs, briefly describe a clinical problem that could be evaluated using any two of the single case designs outlined in the book. Include appropriate diagrams for each of your selections.

Exercise 14.3

Using your current neighborhood or home town as a frame of reference, discuss examples of the different types of needs that current residents might be encountering and tell how these might be evaluated using any two of the different needs assessment strategies discussed in the textbook.

Exercise 14.4

Describe the role of diversity in an agency known to you and discuss in what ways, if any, the Euro-Male paradigm has been dominant in that setting. If you do not yet have experience in an agency setting, you may substitute an organization you are familiar with such as your school, church/temple/mosque.

CHAPTER 15

ANALYZING QUALITATIVE DATA

LEARNING OBJECTIVES

After studying Chapter 15 you will be able to do the following:
1. Describe how quantitative and qualitative data analysis differ from each other;
2. Discuss purpose of the three types of qualitative data coding and the use of analytic memos;
3. Describe at least four different ways to conduct qualitative data analysis;
4. Explain how the absence of something occurring can be highly significant for qualitative analysis;
5. Describe the Method of Agreement and Method of Difference and explain how they can be used together.
6. Explain what an "outcropping" is and how it related to deep, beneath the surface structures.

MATCHING DEFINITIONS

1. A type of qualitative data analysis in which a researcher uses the method of agreement and the method of difference to discover casual factors that affect an outcome among a set of cases.
2. A type of domain based upon the argot and categories used by the people being studied in a field site.
3. A type of domain that in which a researcher uses categories or terms he or she developed to understand a social setting.
4. A type of domain that combines the argot and categories of members under study and the categories developed by a researcher for analysis.
5. A first coding of qualitative data in which a researcher examines the data to condense them into preliminary analytic categories or codes for analyzing the data.
6. A second coding of qualitative data after open coding. The researcher organizes the codes, develops links among them, and discovers key analytic categories.
7. A last pass at coding qualitative data in which a researcher examines previous codes to identify and select illustrative data that will support the conceptual coding categories that he or she developed.
8. A method of qualitative data analysis in which a researcher compares characteristics that are similar across a group of cases, and where the cases share a significant outcome.
9. A method of qualitative data analysis in which a researcher compares the characteristics among cases and where only some cases share a significant outcome, while others do not.
10. A name for conceptual categories in an explanation that a researcher uses as part of the illustrative method of qualitative data analysis.
11. A type of qualitative data analysis that forces a researcher to specify the links among a sequence of many events. It clarifies causal relationships by asking whether one event logically had to follow another, or it just happened to follow.
12. A method of qualitative data analysis in which a researcher describes a domain, or sphere of cultural activities, using the ideas and argot of people in a field site or creates his or her own ideas. The general categories in the domain are cover terms and more specific observations in it are included terms.
13. A method of qualitative data analysis in which a researcher takes the concepts of a social theory or explanation and treats them as empty boxes to be filled with empirical examples and descriptions.

14. Used in <u>domain analysis</u>, a domain is a cultural setting or site in which people regularly interact and develop a set shared understandings or "mini-culture."
15. A method of <u>qualitative data</u> analysis in which the researcher repeatedly moves back and forth between the <u>empirical data</u> and the abstract concepts, theories or models.
16. In the analysis of <u>qualitative data</u>, when a researcher fails to find <u>empirical data</u> on a specific issue, but logically expects such evidence based upon all other evidence and the <u>social theory</u> that the researcher is using.
17. An aspect of <u>qualitative data</u> a researcher recognizes as representing some part of the underlying social structure.

NAME _____ **DATE**

MATCHING KEY TERMS FOR CHAPTER 15

____ Analytic comparison
____ Analytic domain
____ Axial coding
____ Domain
____ Domain analysis
____ Empty boxes
____ Event-Structure Analysis
____ Folk domain
____ llustrative method

____ Method of Agreement
____ Method of Difference
____ Mixed domain
____ Negative evidence
____ Open coding
____ Outcropping
____ Selective Coding
____ Successive approximation

Exercise 15.1

Locate a scholarly article based on qualitative data and provide a photocopy of it. After reading the article answer the following:

1. Did the author use any of the types of qualitative data analysis described in chapter 15 as part of the article? If so which one?

2. Think of an example of a type of event or data which did NOT appear or which did not occur. What did not occur? How would finding such "negative evidence" affect the conclusions of the article?

Exercise 15.2

Identify two folk domains in a social group you have had some contact with. Construct a domain analysis worksheet for each, then do a domain analysis.

Develop at least six included terms in each domain and use a different type of semantic relationship for each domain.

Exercise 15.3

Develop a flowchart of a social activity that you have participated in or will soon participate in (e.g., getting a driver's license, organizing a wedding).   See the example of cake making in the textbook.   In your example include **at least 20 parts** or steps in the process and label them clearly.

12. Deciding whether or not an agency or it's programs are ready for an evaluation is called:
    a. evaluation coverage
    b. gap effectiveness
    c. expected change
    d. evaluability assessment

13. Which of the following is NOT an advantage of the single subject design:
    a. It promotes in-depth qualitative data collection
    b. It is easy to apply in practice settings
    c. It involves little to no statistical testing
    d. Is it minimally disruptive to ordinary practice

14. Process Evaluations have which of the following characteristics?
    a. They answer questions about how the program operates and document the procedures and activities undertaken in service delivery.
    b. They involve the detailed analysis of selected program sites or clients to determine how the interventions or programs are operating, what obstacles to implementation have been experienced, what strategies, if any, have been the most successful in overcoming obstacles.
    c. They have facilitators use an overhead projector, chalkboard , flip-chart so that everyone in a group participates in the ideas presented for all and create a narrative what around group issues deemed by the members to be significant, whether areas of agreement of disagreement.
    d. They address how much the program or program components cost, preferably in relation to alternative uses of the same resources and to the benefits being produced by the program.
    e. They rely almost exclusively on observation and unstructured interviews to study natural settings. They are commonly interested in agency and organizational dynamics

CHAPTER 16

REVIEWING THE LITERATURE AND WRITING A REPORT

LEARNING OBJECTIVES

After studying Chapter 16 you will be able to do the following:
1. Conduct different types of literature reviews and understand the reasons for the differences.
2. Locate information in the scholarly literature using location tools designed for that purpose.
3. Correctly write a bibliographic citation for a scholarly journal using an approved format.
4. Understand the benefits and limits of the Internet for social work research.
5. Explain differences between the basic structure of quantitative and qualitative research reports.
6. Understand the process of grant-writing " and request for proposals.

MATCHING DEFINITIONS

1. A term or word with substantive meaning in a title or about a topic that a researcher uses to locate literature or source related to a topic.
2. A verb that means transferring a computer file from a distant or source computer to a local computer.
3. A type of literature review in which the writer shows how the research design and techniques used to study a topic differ and accounts for discrepancies in findings due to the method used in studies.
4. A term with two meanings in literature reviews: a short summary of a <u>scholarly journal article</u> that usually appears at its beginning, and a reference tool for locating <u>scholarly journal articles</u>.
5. A type of literature review in which the writer blends together several past lines of inquiry into a coherent whole.
6. A type of literature review in which a student demonstrates his or her familiarity with past research to other people, usually teachers.
7. A summary of a research project's findings placed at the beginning of report for an applied, non-specialist audience, usually a little longer than an <u>abstract.</u>
8. A mistake that can occur when writing qualitative research in which a writer separates concrete <u>empirical</u> details from abstract ideas too much.
9. A type of literature review in which the writer traces the development and elaboration of a concept, <u>social theory</u> or theoretical framework.
10. Details of a <u>scholarly journal article</u>'s location that helps people to find it quickly.
11. When a writer restates or rewords the ideas of another person, giving proper credit to the original source.
12. A very early step in the writing process in which the writer tries to get his or her ideas down on paper as quickly as possible, not worrying about grammar or spelling.
13. A literature review in which the writer traces the development of a concept, <u>social theory</u>, or set of findings over time.
14. The person who is primarily in charge of research on a project that is sponsored or funded by an organization.
15. An "address" of an Internet site, usually it begins http://.
16. An announcement by a funding organization that it is willing to fund research and it is soliciting written plans of research projects.

17. A step in the writing process in which the writer goes over a previous draft to improve communication of ideas and clarity of expression.
18. A special type of literature review in which a writer organizes the results from many studies and uses statistical techniques to identify common findings in them.
19. Specialized software to search the Internet using keywords or other information. They return a list of possible Web pages or matching sites.
20. A type of literature review in which the writer places a specific study in a web of previous research and shows the connections from one study to related studies.
21. A "navigational" tool that provides access to the Internet. It is able to interpret various software codes and addresses, and provide screens of information.
22. A writer's temporary inability to write, usually it is psychologically based.
23. A verb that means transferring a computer file from a local computer to a distant computer.

NAME _____ DATE

MATCHING KEY TERMS FOR CHAPTER 16

___ abstract	___ paraphrasing
___ citation	___ principal investigator (PI)
___ context review	___ request for proposals (RFP)
___ download	___ rewriting
___ error of segregation	___ search engine
___ executive summary	___ self-study review
___ freewriting	___ theoretical review
___ historical review	___ Uniform Resource Locator (URL)
___ integrative review	___ upload
___ keyword	___ web browser
___ meta-analysis	___ writer's block
___ methodological review	

Exercise 16.1

Determine whether your college or university has an office devoted to research grants (sometimes called sponsored research or extramural research). Visit the office in person or on-line and ask how you could find two **Request For Proposals** for a topic for a professor/teacher that you know. Get all the documentation for the RFP's including length, outline, etc. that may be required. Ideally, get RFP's issued by two different funding organizations or agencies so you can compare them. If the office has a copy of a full grant proposal that has been submitted, whether or not it has been funded, ask if you can borrow it. From the two RFP's and the grant proposal, answer the following questions:
- What evidence, if any, is there that the author should be familiar with the scholarly literature on a topic.
- How detailed is the description of the process of doing the research that is being proposed?
- What HumanSubjects and IRB issues were involved? How were they addressed?
- How important does the background of the person going to do the research appear to be.
- Does budget part of the proposals seem to be very relevant?

NOTES

NOTES

NOTES

NOTES

NOTES

NOTES

NOTES

NOTES

NOTES

NOTES